Langston Hughes and American Lynching Culture

UNIVERSITY PRESS OF FLORIDA

Florida A&M University, Tallahassee
Florida Atlantic University, Boca Raton
Florida Gulf Coast University, Ft. Myers
Florida International University, Miami
Florida State University, Tallahassee
New College of Florida, Sarasota
University of Central Florida, Orlando
University of Florida, Gainesville
University of North Florida, Jacksonville
University of South Florida, Tampa
University of West Florida, Pensacola

Langston Hughes

University Press of Florida
Gainesville
Tallahassee
Tampa
Boca Raton
Pensacola
Orlando
Miami
Jacksonville
Ft. Myers
Sarasota

American
Lynching
Culture

and

W. Jason Miller

First cloth printing, 2011
First paperback printing, 2012

LIBRARY OF CONGRESS CATALOGING-IN-PUBLICATION DATA
Miller, W. Jason.
Langston Hughes and American lynching culture / W. Jason Miller.
p. cm.
Includes bibliographical references and index.
ISBN 978-0-8130-3533-8 (alk. paper)
ISBN 978-0-8130-4152-0 (pbk.)
1. Hughes, Langston, 1902–1967—Criticism and interpretation. 2. Hughes, Langston,
1902–1967—Political and social views. 3. Hughes, Langston, 1902–1967—Political
activity. 4. Lynching in literature. 5. African Americans in literature. 6. Lynching—
United States—History. I. Title.
PS3515.U274Z6843 2010
811.'5209—dc22   2010023264

The University Press of Florida is the scholarly publishing agency for the State
University System of Florida, comprising Florida A&M University, Florida Atlantic
University, Florida Gulf Coast University, Florida International University, Florida
State University, New College of Florida, University of Central Florida, University
of Florida, University of North Florida, University of South Florida, and University
of West Florida.

University Press of Florida
15 Northwest 15th Street
Gainesville, FL 32611-2079
http://www.upf.com

In remembrance of all those who have refused the bitter cup filled with gall and to all the others who have unwittingly accepted the same cup and swallowed.

Contents

Figures

Acknowledgments

While this project is a testament to my own growing understanding of Hughes's poetry, it is also the result of much-needed guidance, encouragement, and refinement from many other people. I am especially grateful to Camille Roman, Professor Emeritus, Washington State University. Her editorial and organizational suggestions have shaped the very best that this book has to offer.

During this project's genesis in Pullman, Washington, I also benefited from the generosity of numerous other scholars. Alex Hammond deepened my awareness of Hughes while simultaneously opening up new approaches to this material. I also offer my thanks to George Kennedy and Victor Villanueva, heads of Washington State's Department of English.

The evolution of *Langston Hughes and American Lynching Culture* was similarly influenced by the University Press of Florida. It is rare to be extended the privilege of working with an ideal editor, but Amy Gorelick was that and more. Amy served a primary role in locating the very best elements of my ideas and demonstrated tireless effort to secure prompt feedback that enabled the project to gain momentum at every stage.

A Yemisi Jimoh and Anne Rice proved to be the most astute readers for which a writer could hope. Each read and responded to this manuscript with inspiring attentiveness and rhetorical prowess. I would also like to thank each dedicated member of the staff at the University Press of Florida. Susan Murray also provided remarkable clarity to this work.

I am also indebted to other colleagues who provided me with opportunities to present many of the materials that appear in the first two chapters at various intellectual forums. Thomas Travisano kindly invited me to attend the "Elizabeth Bishop and Her Worlds" international symposium in December 2003, which gave me the opportunity to bring Hughes's "The Bitter River" into a critical conversation with Bishop's "Santarém." The Langston Hughes Society and Dolan Hubbard tendered a keen audience and large forum for discussing Hughes's "The Negro Speaks of Rivers." My good fortune to appear as part of a panel sponsored by the Langston Hughes Society at the Modern Language Association in 2004 brought me into scholarly conversation with such devoted Hughes scholars as Donna Akiba Sullivan Harper and R. Baxter Miller. Moreover, serving as part of a dynamic panel organized by Sandra Staton-Taiwu at the NEMLA conference in 2006 gave me the opportunity to test and share materials surrounding "Christ in Alabama." I also had the good fortune of being a panelist at the 2007 American Literature Association annual convention. Here, Matthew Hofer and Scarlet Higgins offered insight and frames of reference that pushed my thinking forward.

It is with humility that I thank the *Langston Hughes Review*. In particular, R. Baxter Miller and Valerie Babb have significantly sharpened the clarity of my writing.

Among my admittedly limited circle of friends, Angie Oberg emerged as a highly coveted reader who willingly offered time, suggestions, and insight. I thank her for her expertise, jovial commentaries, and suggestions.

This project never would have been completed without the unparalleled assistance of faculty members in North Carolina State University's Department of English. Department heads Antony Harrison, Mary Helen Thuente, and Walt Wolfram secured important travel funding. I am grateful to the vast array of our department's astute and generous colleagues.

Serving as a remarkably careful and detailed research assistant, Laura White showed impressive instincts and tact in winnowing through primary sources that proved essential. Melissa Couchon's and Rebecca le Roux's attentive eyes have made them the most trustworthy of editorial assistants. A special thanks for making me more placewise belongs to Alice Osborn, whose interest in Hughes's poetry offered valuable insight into the spatial dynamics of Mississippi.

I thank all the undergraduate and graduate students who listened with patience and interest as I worked through the complexities of Hughes's "Dream Deferred."

▶•◀

I am also grateful to the Southern Historical Collection, University of North Carolina–Chapel Hill, for permission to quote material from the archives; the Allen-Littlefield Collection for use of the photographs reproduced in chapter 1; Tammy Carter at the Collection Center for Creative Photography, University of Arizona, for permission to reproduce two of Marion Palfi's photographs; the archives at North Carolina State University, for access to various out-of-print materials; the Associated Press, for the image of Langston Hughes testifying before HUAC; Fordham University Press, for permission to reproduce Prentiss Taylor's lithograph. Some of the ideas in chapter 1 were published earlier in a different form, and I am grateful for the permission granted by the *Langston Hughes Review* to develop them further here.

Also, special thanks for use of "The Bitter River," "Christ in Alabama," "Mississippi," "The Negro Speaks of Rivers," from *The Collected Poems of Langston Hughes* by Langston Hughes, edited by Arnold Rampersad with David Roessel, Associate Editor, copyright © 1994 by the Estate of Langston Hughes. Used by permission of Alfred A. Knopf, a division of Random House, Inc. These poems are also reprinted by permission of Harold Ober Associates Incorporated.

Notwithstanding the gracious support I have received from all the colleagues mentioned above, any and all mistakes herein are mine and mine alone.

▶•◀

Finally, I wish to thank my family. I appreciate my parents' unquestioned support. My son, Austin, has grown tall during my extended periods of writing. Please accept my gratitude for your patience. Without question, my deepest gratitude goes to my wife, Sherri. I thank her for supporting me unconditionally despite all the months she was made to feel like an interruption. My truest expressions of thanks cannot come in written form; such reverence can best be expressed in person. For now, please let these printed words suffice: her only peers are saints.

When I was a child, headlines in the colored papers used to scare the daylights out of me. I grew up in Kansas and for years I was afraid to go down South, thinking—as a result of the Negro press—that I might be lynched the minute I got off the train.

Langston Hughes, from a speech at the Windy City Press Club Banquet, January 10, 1957

Introduction

Langston Hughes never lived in an America where the very real threat of lynching did not exist. He died in 1967, a year before the last officially recorded lynching. Lynching had a direct impact on Hughes's life and creative works. As Langston Hughes's above comment reminds us, his earliest engagement with lynching came through reading about it as a child. However, his engagement did not end there. These fears accompanied him during his first trip by train through the South when he was a teenager. Moreover, he repeatedly responded to lynching throughout his creative works for the remainder of his life. Revisiting his published poems reveals an important current in American cultural history.

Langston Hughes engaged in a lifelong national campaign against American lynching culture. In fact, Hughes addressed, referenced, responded, or alluded to lynching in nearly three dozen different poems. This project uses Hughes's campaign as a context for reading seven of his most important poetic responses to lynching, which reveal the complex interplay between culture, politics, and art. Among other techniques, this study uses cultural studies, biographical information, and textual criticism to better understand these works. This study not only reconstructs Hughes's neglected lifelong campaign against lynching, but it also provides an unprecedented opportunity to see how lynching affected one writer throughout the course of his life. Hughes's lifetime, from 1902 to 1967, parallels a critical era in American history. This study of Hughes's poetry initiates an important dialogue in the relationship between America's neglected history of sadistic torture and some of the world's most significant poems. It also amplifies a variety of inflections surrounding the practice of lynching in twentieth-century America.

Hughes's national campaign against lynching has not been explored adequately. In order to understand how Hughes addressed lynching throughout his poetry, it is important to understand the history of lynching. It has taken a long time for Americans to think about lynching, and names such as Ida B. Wells-Barnett, Walter White, and Billie Holiday are more commonly linked to this subject. It was Wells who first retraced the original press coverage and horrific stories of lynching. Her book *On Lynchings* finds no fewer than twenty thousand people attending some public lynchings (31). Several of the incidents she records occurred outside the South. Much later, the New York exhibit in 2000 of James Allen's collection of lynching photographs ushered in a new awareness of lynching. Leon Litwack's introduction to *Without Sanctuary*, the book of photographs that resulted from this exhibit, offers the following story as representational of what might happen to a lynch victim. This is what happened to Sam Hose when he was lynched in Newman, Georgia:

> After stripping Hose of his clothes and chaining him to a tree, the self-appointed executioners stacked kerosene-soaked wood high around him. Before saturating Hose with oil and applying the torch, they cut off his ears, fingers, and genitals, and skinned his face. While some in the crowd plunged knives into the victim's flesh, others watched "with unfeinging [*sic*] satisfaction" (as one reporter noted) the contortions of Sam Hose's body as the flames rose distorting his features, causing his eyes to bulge out of their sockets, and rupturing his veins. . . . Before Hose's body had even cooled, his heart and liver were removed and cut into several pieces and his bones were crushed into small particles. The crowd fought over these souvenirs. (9)

It is important to remember that lynchings occurred throughout the twentieth century in the North and the South. It is estimated that at least 4,742 blacks were lynched between 1882 and 1968 (Litwack 12). It is in the middle of this literary and political history that all of Hughes's poetry is located.

Lynching

The word "lynching" has been used in many ways. In the eighteenth century, some used the term to designate the punishment assigned to a horse thief who received "thirty-nine blows to the back" (Gussow 52). In Virginia, Judge Charles Lynch reportedly punished Tories during the American Revolution, and "lynch law" was "understood to be execution without due process of the law" (Apel 23). By 1922, the term "lynching" was defined in antilynching legislation as "five or more persons acting in concert for the purpose of depriving any person his life without authority of law" (Dray viii). Failed antilynching legislation continued to refine its definitions so that the number of people who constituted a "mob" was eventually reduced from five to three to two people between 1922 and 1950 (Dray viii).

This relatively rapid revision of the definition of lynching reminds us that lynching often means many different things. Some people have speculated that the varying forms of violence defined as lynching may suggest that "the history of lynching possesses too great a burden for any one word to carry" (Goldsby 282). To clarify these forms, I discuss lynching in four general ways. The story of Sam Hose serves as an example of *spectacle lynching*. Crowds numbering in the thousands witnessed such lynchings on courthouse lawns, where advertisements often drew witnesses who traveled to the announced event by train. I also discuss a second form of lynching known as *mob lynching*. Although spectacle lynching was advertised, lynchings also occurred at the hands of angry mobs. Appearing to be more spontaneously organized, these groups sometimes stormed jail cells or victims' homes, with the lynching occurring later the same day.

Because Hughes himself addresses lynching in a third way in his poetry, I also discuss *legal lynchings*. While, at the very least, "4,742 blacks met their deaths at the hands of lynch mobs . . . [a]s many if not more blacks were victims of legal lynchings (speedy trials and executions)" (Litwack 12). Hughes's response to the Scottsboro case of 1931 reminds us that there were also numerous successful attempts to stage legal lynchings.

By midcentury, bombings, shootings, and other forms of intimidation and murder terrorized African American victims and communities. *Domestic terrorism* is a fourth term that can be used to discuss lynching. Hughes used the term "terror" himself in his 1955 response to the lynching of Emmett Till, and the term's present cultural currency accurately evokes the fear and intimidation intended by American lynching culture.

Lynchings affected victims, near victims, survivors, and communities, and further encouraged and inaugurated new discriminators with a value system that privileged power. Literature, mass media, and politics reflect its legacy. To capture what lynching meant in varying arenas, I extend my focus beyond the act of lynching itself. Lynching is more than an act of violence; it demands that we focus our attention on its vast interconnections with American culture. To discuss the implications of lynching that extend well beyond the moment in which a murder is committed, I refer to American lynching culture. The phrase "American lynching culture" is intended to capture the varying inflections of lynching that saturated the literal and cultural landscape of the United States throughout the twentieth century. It suggests, in very broad strokes, that lynching is a uniquely American practice that was enacted, sustained, and tolerated by a complex interplay of socioeconomic, psychological, racial, sexual, and political motives. Of course, this phrase has limitations that stem mostly from the broad range of drives it seeks to capture and engage. It is a difficult burden for any paradigm to fully account for this vast range of interconnections. The phrase represents a desire to recognize and account for the wide range of factors that surrounded lynching in America. In one way or another, the phrase allows this work to make cultural interconnections in regard to how lynching affected victims and survivors, artists and editors, writers and readers, bystanders and perpetrators. Interlocking these perspectives amplifies Hughes's broad cultural engagement with these varying groups.

Although lynching has a long history in America, it was primarily a postbellum phenomenon. Tuskegee Institute began keeping official statistics of lynchings in 1882. In the first year, the confirmed cases showed that more whites than blacks were among the casualties. Only four years later, the counts were reversed as frontier justice quickly turned this extralegal means toward controlling black citizens. In

1892, more than 161 blacks were lynched. Lynching numbers remained extremely high well into the twentieth century. In 1919, eighty-three African Americans were reported to have been lynched. By the early twentieth century, African American men had become the main targets of American lynching culture as they represented the strongest threat to dominant culture. This trend continued throughout the century.[1]

Exactly how lynching became so deeply rooted in America is a subject still being explored by cultural historians. William Carrigan has recently defined four historical developments most responsible for shaping the cultural acceptance of lynching from 1836 to 1919. Though his study focuses on Texas, these principles apply to many other regions of America, too. First, the realities of frontier life were essential in "forming ideas about the necessity of vigilantism and extralegal violence" (12). Varying conflicts (both real and imagined) between outlaws, land-hungry settlers, Mexicans, Native Americans, and black citizens revealed the limitations of the "state's still-developing legal system" (12). Hence, regulation fell to local citizens, and patterns of unregulated violence became so common that they became accepted. Second, slavery "undermined the formal legal system" by allowing slave owners and overseers the power of "investigation, judgment, and sentencing of many crimes" (13). This is especially relevant to the lynching of African American men. Third, understandable resistance by "racial, ethnic, and political minorities" heightened the intensity of conflict as people with differing interests competed for control. Fourth, and finally, as more formal courts emerged, law officers simply continued to tolerate lynching because the "attitudes of local authorities" wielding power were shaped by the cultural memories they had inherited and grown accustomed to enforcing (13).

From this point forward in American history, the long acceptance of lynching continued to accomplish many things simultaneously. This practice extended well beyond the realm of enforcers and victims. For Langston Hughes, encountering American lynching culture in his youth required a steadying of nerves; his response later intensified into anger as this travesty of American justice was hypocritically tolerated by the masses. This culture also sought to silence Hughes's critiques of lynching, and Hughes was faced with the prospect of negotiating not only the act of lynching but also the complicated political climate that sought to curb his ability to discuss it in poetry. American lynching culture called for varying responses among survivors and accomplices. Acts of resistance or acceptance are just a few of the responses made by people who lived in such a climate.

Justifying the current need for such a study of lynching is regrettably easy, as its impact on American identity is far from ending. In fact, varying inflections of lynching still exist today throughout American culture. The deaths of Matthew Shepard and James Byrd Jr. in 1998, the inordinately high percentages of black inmates to receive capital punishment, and practices that violate the Geneva Convention at such known sites as Abu Ghraib, Guantanamo Bay, and Bagram Air Base confirm the continuation of a uniquely American strain of torture, violence, and murder. Moreover, the hanging deaths of Raynard Johnson in 2000, Stanley Forestal in 2002, Leonard Gakinya in 2002, and Ferris Golden in 2003 were "quickly ruled suicides by local authorities, a verdict that was openly disputed by the families" (Apel 16). In addition, serious complaints of harassment in the workplace continue to invoke the memory of lynching. A $1.82 million lawsuit was brought against a Chicago-based company whose employees displayed nooses in May 2002, and another $1 million suit was filed against Adelphia Communications in Miami when a manager placed a noose in his office on a daily basis and then moved it to the doorway on "Bring Your Child to Work Day" (Apel 16–17). These examples are hardly unique. In fact, thirteen different nooses were uncovered at the Atlanta-based Georgia Power Company between 1998 and 2004.

Most recently, a group of six students ranging from the ages of fifteen to seventeen were arrested in December 2006 in Louisiana. Referred to as the Jena Six, these young men were involved in an altercation at their high school. Earlier in the school year, no action was taken when three nooses were found hanging from a prominent tree located on school property. The day before the nooses were discovered, a black student had formally requested permission to sit under the tree that everyone understood was to be used exclusively by white students. Finally, the words "Hang Obama by a noose" were spray-painted on a tunnel located on the campus of North Carolina State University on November 5, 2008. The writing was found the morning after Barack Obama had won the presidential election. After the students apologized for their language, no action was taken against them because the words had been included in what the university had designated as a "Free Expression Tunnel."

It should be acknowledged that these linkages create complex problems in analysis, as office bullying and geopolitics function on very different planes. In listing these diverse examples here, I seek only to express and expose how broad the spectrum is for recognizing lynching's continuing impact in America. American lynching culture still has varying impacts on instigators, victims, and people who imagine they are sheltered by apathy or indifference. Consensus, observation, awareness, and acceptance continue to penetrate to the deepest levels of American culture. There is convincing evidence that the logic of lynching will continue to reemerge, and that the less the subject of lynching is understood, the more potent it becomes.

Langston Hughes

Considering that lynching itself emerged in many forms throughout the twentieth century, it is not surprising to find that Hughes's responses to it varied and evolved. Hughes addressed, referenced, responded, or alluded to lynching throughout the course of his life as a poet. Each of Hughes's poetic references to lynching, as well as several appearances of this subject in his plays, operas, newspaper articles, short stories, and histories are addressed within this study. However, I have devoted most of my energy to building substantial cultural contexts for seven of Hughes's most noteworthy and complex poetic responses. The poems on which I focus have achieved a well-deserved and sustainable canonicity to which this study contributes. Moreover, their importance is still growing. These poems are indispensable statements, necessary for understanding a powerful current that runs through the works of one of the most prolific writers of the twentieth century.

As such, this study contributes to varying academic fields. The contributions to Hughes scholarship made by Arnold Rampersad and Steven Tracy, which have established the biographical and musical significance of Hughes, are key touchstones that inform the framework of the present work. I also build on the fact that Hughes has been established as an important voice of the Left in the significant critical work of Christopher C. De Santis, Donna Akiba Sullivan Harper, Susan Duffy, and Jonathan Scott. This work on Hughes's essays, the Simple stories, political plays, and methods of communicating socialist joy have offered the kinds of illuminating insights I seek to extend. With each of these voices, I, too, seek to affirm that Hughes was "committed to the possibilities of language to generate social awareness and ultimately, to compel social change" (De Santis 304).

Yet literary scholarship has been noticeably silent about one subject that consumed Hughes throughout the entire course of his career. In fact, this book is the first full-length study devoted to any one writer's lifelong responses to the subject of lynching. Hughes's responses to lynching comprise a key inflection in our still-emerging conceptualizations of African American literature, culture, and modernity. I hope to counter the volatility of this subject matter by avoiding sensationalism and, instead, engaging the social complexities of lynching. Hughes's poems that address American lynching culture exemplify his dynamic relationship with politics and culture.

Topophilia and Topophobia

In order to better illuminate this subject, I incorporate several methods of inquiry. These methods vary in accordance with Hughes's evolving responses to lynching's shifting trajectories. Before we turn to the work that demonstrates Hughes's varying responses to American lynching culture, an explanation of why I focus some of my early discussion on Hughes's use of river imagery may be helpful. Lynchings often occurred at rivers, where victims were hung from suspension bridges. These riverscapes are especially rife with historical and cultural significance, and a historically informed use of an ecocritical lens is warranted. Elizabeth Dodd has demonstrated the implications of placing Michael Harper's speaker near a swamp in his poem "History as Apple Picking." After tracing the history of the word "swamp" to colonial America, "specifically Virginia," Dodd finds that the swamps themselves are filled with important "Anglo-colonial attitudes towards land" (188). The swamps are read as "the literal testing grounds for American economic identity and race policy," which Harper is intent on trying to access (188). For Hughes, the Mississippi River mentioned in "The Negro Speaks of Rivers" is an intimidating site he needs to master as he travels toward Texas by train in the Red Summer of 1919. Crossing the Mississippi places Hughes closer to Texas. During this time, Texas was one of the "many theaters in which brutalized black male bodies—sometimes nude, often bullet-ridden—were put on display, then reported in the black press with vividness and outrage" (Gussow 181). Likewise, the Chickasawhay River mentioned in "The Bitter River" is a place that needs to be remembered for the lynchings that occurred there rather than for the architectural engineering that placed the Shubuta Bridge that crosses it on the National Register of Historic Sites in 1988.

To help read Hughes more deeply, I also consider his poetry in terms of topophilia and topophobia. Highlighting the important work of cultural geographers, each of these terms can be applied to the way we anticipate, experience, and remember places. "Topophilia," a term that captures the affection a person connects to a place, comes in varying degrees. It includes high expectations of enjoyment that accompany travel, active engagement with an environment that creates wonder or new knowledge for the participant, and the nostalgic images that remind us of the pleasure experienced at a particular site. More specifically, in "The Negro Speaks of Rivers," Hughes transcends time and culture by seeking to enjoy riverscapes as others have enjoyed them.

"Topophobia" is my term for summing up the various fears we associate with places. Examples include particular anxieties that range from feeling uncomfortable to concerns about being lynched. A general example would be preferring urban places over rural ones. Because place experiences stay with us, topophobia reveals itself in potent forms. Despite its close connections with irrational behavior, my use of "phobia" here does not suggest that these fears are without due cause. Quite the opposite, my exploration of topophobia seeks to capture the hidden basis for justifiable responses of fear.

Even toponymns are significant for understanding topophobia. For example, Hughes's later revisions of "The Negro" place lynching in Mississippi as opposed to earlier versions that instead mention Texas. Among other things, the name change reminds us that, at different times in the twentieth century, simple references to state names would instill potent images of lynching in readers' minds.

In the face of topophobia, there is a need to reassure and calm oneself. In addition to altering the way we actively perceive things, feelings of topophobia inevitably occur in realizing that places have more cultural history than we can ever adequately recover or artistically represent. I contend that feelings of topophobia and topophilia need to be sifted because they are often intermingled within the same poem. Hence, Hughes's "The Negro Speaks of Rivers" expresses a longing to recapture an intimate relationship with riverscapes at a moment when Hughes is also most fearful of the violence that can occur there.

Passing

In order to better understand Hughes's varied responses to American lynching culture, I use the term "passing." "Passing" is sometimes used socially to denote a black person passing for white. In his short 1950 essay "Fooling Our White Folks," Hughes describes the most obvious form of passing for readers of the *Negro Digest*: "For those who are able to do it, passing for white is, of course, the most common means of escaping color handicaps. . . . The consensus of opinion among Negroes seems to be approval of those who can get by with it. Almost all of us know Negroes of light complexion who, during the war, were hustled through their draft boards so fast they were unwittingly put into white units and did their service entirely without the humiliations of the military color bar" (*CW* 9: 314). Hughes also conveys his overall attitude toward such passing: "because our American whites are stupid in many ways, racially speaking, and because there are many things in the U.S.A. of ours which Negroes may achieve only by guile, I have great tolerance for persons of color who deliberately set out to fool our white folks" (*CW* 9: 314).

Hughes then outlines three distinct ways to pass. These three techniques are important to this study because each was invoked by Hughes at various times during his interactions with American lynching culture. First, Hughes suggests that complicating issues of nationality can be just as successful as having a light complexion. Hughes tells of a friend who, though too dark to pass for white, entered a Greek restaurant only to be told he would not be served. The friend responded: "but did you never hear of Socrates? He was a black Greek. Many noble Greeks of old were colored. I am descended from such ancient Greeks. What do you mean, I, a black Greek, cannot eat here?" (*CW* 9: 316). This friend reports that he was allowed to eat without any further complaints from the owners.

The use of humor shown here is a second means by which to successfully escape some acts of racism. Hughes relates a personal vignette of sitting in the white section of an Alabama diner. When asked by "the white steward" if he was "Negro or foreign," he simply replied, "I'm just hungry!" evoking laughter from all the black workers in the car (*CW* 9: 316). Hughes was soon served.

Third and finally, Hughes tells his readers to be a "little daring" with language when he states that "'Dame un boletto [*sic*] Pullman to Chicago,' will get you a berth in Texas when often plain English, 'Give me a Pullman ticket to Chicago,' will not" (*CW* 9: 316). Hughes suggests altering linguistic performance, by which white listeners "are very easily fooled. . . . But since they are prejudiced, there's no harm in fooling the devil, is there?" (*CW* 9: 317).

Although Hughes uses the term "passing" in the most general sense as a means to escape all forms of racism, I am appropriating and narrowing the parameters of the term in this study to discuss how Hughes interacted with American lynching culture. As I discuss at length in chapter 1, Hughes's example of complicating his nationality and language by passing as Mexican secured him a Pullman berth during his first trip through Texas in 1919. This berth did more than offer him a more comfortable ride than the one afforded back on the Jim Crow cars: it lessened his chances of being a victim of violence. Furthermore, Hughes invoked humor to significantly lessen community outrage on the campus of the University of North Carolina at Chapel Hill in 1931. Such humor was imperative. In fact, police were called in to stand guard around the doors of Gerrard Hall to calm the angry crowd who had just read "Christ in Alabama" after it appeared on the front page of a local magazine earlier that day. This legal force was ultimately unnecessary because all tension was dissolved by Hughes's own ability to make the audience laugh throughout his opening remarks that evening.

Examples of passing have often been invoked to negotiate American lynching culture. Hughes himself praised Walter White in "Ballad of Walter White" (1941) for his ability to investigate lynchings because his complexion enabled him to *pass*. Elisabeth Freeman passed during the process of collecting information for her article on the lynching of Jesse Washington that later appeared in *Crisis*. She secured information about the incident from Judge Munrow by passing: "When I met with him the second time, with different clothes on, he did not recognize me. I put on a strong English accent. . . . Then he gave me the court records" ("The Waco Horror" 6).

Among other incidents, the lynching of Lemuel Walters in Longview, Texas, in 1919 resulted in a sustained resistance by blacks in the community. One leader, fearing for his own safety after the resistance led to the deaths of eleven white men, "disguised himself as a soldier, boarded a train, rode a short distance and dismounted" ("The Riot at Longview, Texas" 298).

Because the cultural climate surrounding Hughes shifted at various times in his life, Hughes's attempts at passing were sometimes negotiated against the combined social force of American lynching culture and red-baiting. In the postwar era, censorship and repeated accusations of communism gained increasing force from J. Edger Hoover. Such authority simultaneously hindered and marshaled Hughes's creative energies. Hughes's postwar poetry was twice as volatile, as he was coded both black and red.

Passing helps us understand how Hughes accomplished the task of veiling the subject of lynching in his 1959 edition of "The Negro" when red-baiting limited his responses to anti-American commentary. Hughes, forced to negotiate censorship, revised "The Negro" for his *Selected Poems* of 1959 and even read it out loud in Washington, D.C., in 1962. With other poems, he accomplished this miraculous achievement by "articulating other voices with such force and clarity that readers have assumed his complete disappearance from the poem" (Ponce 528). However, with "The Negro," Hughes created the illusion that he was only retelling history. By framing his criticism of contemporary lynching in a poem that seemed only to recount history, Hughes was able to pass this brief but potent critique of lynching.

I am intentionally highlighting the interconnectedness of the personal and literary moments where Hughes passed. In fact, the ability to physically pass informed Hughes's guile to successfully pass his literary statements about lynching. Essentially Hughes's ability to pass embraces the social power of signifying. The use of passing can be understood as a specific type of signifying or masking aimed exclusively at a culture recognized internationally for lynching its black citizens. Because Hughes used the term "passing" specifically, because my use of the term is limited to negotiating lynching, and because Hughes's personal experiences of physically passing evolved into literary stealth, I use the term "passing" rather than the closely related terms "signifying" or "masking." In person, Hughes passed through American lynching culture and red-baiting by complicating his nationality, using humor effectively, and manipulating language. In poetry, he also negotiated varying aspects of censorship by retelling history.

Negotiating Censorship

Hughes engaged the strategy of retelling history to pass one of his poems about American lynching culture on to the general public in the 1950s. This strategy was effective in "The Negro," where Hughes invoked the "quasi-(in)visible dissent" practiced in the "rewriting" of "specific historical or cultural events" (Roman 4). By appearing only to retell past history, this poem reads like a narrative account bent on recovering cultural memories rather than an angry protest pushing for immediate social or legislative change. His strategy worked because the poem spends eighteen of its nineteen lines referencing a history that happened in the distant past and only one short line commenting on the contemporary subject of lynching. This strategy extended Hughes's creativity as he was able to subtly yet clearly address the realities of American lynching culture at a time when his cultural status earned his poems increased scrutiny during the height of anti-communist paranoia.

Counternarrative

Like so many other writers, Hughes recognized early on that mainstream daily newspapers offered inadequate representations of lynching. Hughes took several opportunities to offer counternarratives to these newspaper reports in his short stories, plays, and poetry. Among others, his short story "Father and Son" (1934), play *Don't You Want to Be Free?* (1943), and poem "Mississippi" (1955) serve as artistic correctives to the incomplete accounts told by the press. The historical recovery of the way lynchings were covered by the press suggests that "lynching was one of those experiences reporters were not allowed to represent fully, naturally it fell to writers of fiction, not journalists, to do it justice. . . . [L]ynching can be understood as one of those pressing topics that literature took up when journalism fell short" (Lutes 457).

With "Father and Son," Hughes subverted newsprint sources by contrasting his narrative with a newspaper account of a lynching he included in the final paragraph of the story. Hughes's story and the newspaper clipping contradict each other, and Hughes takes the inaccurate article and sets his own text against it. Here, literature offers the emotional background and accuracy lacking in mainstream accounts of lynchings. More telling still is Hughes's literary response to the lynching of Emmett Till in 1955. Rather than responding to the lynching of fourteen-year-old Till as an isolated incident, Hughes places his murder against the context of all the unknown lynch victims who have died in Mississippi. This form of counternarrative serves as a reminder that what happened to the visiting Till had been happening to residents of Mississippi for decades.

Photography

Visual imagery is also important for understanding Hughes's engagement with American lynching culture. Illustrations that accompanied Hughes's poetry serve as key contexts for interpretation. It should be remembered that more of Hughes's poems appeared with illustrations than the poems of any other poet in the twentieth century (Axelrod, Roman, and Travisano 694). In particular, images by Zell Ingram and Prentiss Taylor, which accompanied "Christ in Alabama" (1931), illuminate the context of the Scottsboro case that inspired Hughes's poem. Hughes's connection to the visual medium has previously been explored by Jonathan Scott and Michael Thurston. Scott examines three of Hughes's anthologies to suggest that "A new concept—the 'collage aesthetic'—can be used to account for the logic and direction of Hughes's astonishingly diverse literary output during the cold war (165–66). Thurston builds off the realm of cinema to suggest the possibility for readers to create "textual montages that draw their discrete shots from more widely disparate realms" ("Montage of a Dream Destroyed" 206). Rather than applying either of these very portable approaches to Hughes's work as an editor or to seeing ways in which Hughes's images collide with others to mimic small films, I extend part of my discussion of Hughes's use of visual elements in relation to photography.

In one instance, Hughes's topophobic anticipations of Texas are sharpened as a result of viewing the photographs of Jesse Washington's lynching in a 1916 edition of *Crisis*. Six photos in this article capture the horrific burning and dismemberment of Washington's body during a lynching that lasted no fewer than five hours. The impact was felt by Hughes, who reminds us that "I learned to read with *The Crisis* on my Grandmother's lap" (CW 10: 197).

Hughes's ability to blur photographic representation into poetic imagery continued its maturation and reached its climax during the postwar era. Rather than use "collage" or "montage" to discuss Hughes's poetic practice, I invoke the term "photo-text" to understand specific poems created by Hughes. My use of the term "photo-text" is intended to invoke the work of Sara Blair, who has argued that as the use of photography in postwar America increased, African American authors "test[ed] the powers of their art in a landscape increasingly shaped by visual texts and visuality" (18). It is important to remember that Hughes "worked (sometimes simultaneously) with photojournalists, documentary agencies, and some of the most celebrated art photographers of the post-war era" (Blair xviii–xix). Some of these photographers included Roy DeCarava, Henri Cartier-Bresson, Griffith J. Davis, and Marion Palfi.

Finally, in the exchange between the seeing eye of photography and the spoken words of poetry, no photographic image need accompany a written text. As Blair has demonstrated, Ralph Ellison's "*Invisible Man* becomes at its climax a photo-text without photographs, a text both indebted to and exceeding the cultural genres shaping the era and its emergence" (149). In other words, texts were written for a culture that was increasing its visual literacy. For Hughes, such viewers animated new opportunities for infusing linguistic imagery, simile, and metaphor into the visual and verbal space made possible by photography's increasing influence as a mode of knowing. Just as important, there is an inherent ambiguity that accompanies visual imagery. This mode of writing ripened in Hughes's work during the period when he was forced to negotiate censorship. In response, he activated the idea of lynching as a useful analogy.

Chapter Previews

Given the shifting cultural contexts of Hughes's life and the ever-changing forms of lynching, this work follows a chronological sequence in addressing Hughes's poetry. The first chapter offers a rereading of "The Negro Speaks of Rivers" within the context of spectacle lynching. Hughes composed his first and most widely known poem while riding on a train headed through Texas during the Red Summer of 1919. As such, the contemporaneous lynchings of Jesse Washington and Lige Daniels, as well as the Longview Race Riot, are discussed as examples of the dangers awaiting the young Hughes as he traveled through the South. The poem is an example of what kind of art is produced when an artist is asked to pass through the shadow of traumatic dismemberment. In this poem, Hughes overcomes feelings of topophobia to find and record his self-reassurance in the face of American lynching culture. By reading "The Negro Speaks of Rivers" beyond the boundaries of its archetypal speaker, Hughes's personal role in the composition of the poem becomes amplified. Read within the context of lynching, it records how Hughes calmed his fears against the threat of physical danger.

In chapter 2, I discuss the Scottsboro case of 1931 and the continued failure to pass antilynching laws in the United States throughout the 1940s. During this time, Hughes was overt in his resistance to and anger against the practice of lynching. Hughes's response to the Scottsboro case resulted in "Christ in Alabama," a poem that characterizes the Scottsboro trials as a form of legal lynching. The depth of its controversial imagery is documented in regard to the direct impact it had on immediate advertising losses suffered by its first publisher. In addition, the hypocrisy of fighting against racism abroad during World War II serves as a cultural context for reading "The Bitter River." Hughes penned one of the longest poems of his career in response to the lynchings of two fourteen-year-old boys, Ernest Green and Charlie Lang. The interplay and shifts from place affection to place fear are considered here in addition to the details surrounding this lynching and others that occurred earlier at this same location. The poem reminds us that remembering the past acts of lynching must be painful.

The third chapter introduces the 1950s as a time when Hughes was forced to negotiate censorship in greater intensity. This period also marked a time when forms of lynching were again changing. In this climate, Hughes explored the use of lynching as an analogy. Two poems, "Not for Publication" and "Dream Deferred," are closely examined. Hughes addressed the figurative lynching that awaited those people who spoke out about racism in "Not for Publication," and Hughes's own interrogation before HUAC, the lynching of Harry Moore, and the case of Paul Robeson are considered as cultural parallels for the points Hughes makes in this poem. Hughes's relationship with photographers Roy DeCarava, Henri Cartier-Bresson, Griffith J. Davis, and Marion Palfi inform this reading of "Dream Deferred." The use of food imagery in this poem asks us to consider whether Hughes used lynching as an analogy in this poem. Imagery itself becomes an important register in which poetry becomes more akin to photography's ability to show in pictures what cannot be said in words.

Chapter 4 examines two of Hughes's closely related pair of texts—"The Negro" and "Mississippi"—both of which shift Hughes's poetic associations with lynching from Texas to the Mississippi Delta. In "The Negro," Hughes applied the skills of passing in person to the ability to pass poems into print. Hughes passed an important revision of "The Negro" in an important reading in Washington, D.C., as well as into his heavily censored *Selected Poems* via the guise of retelling history. Moreover, Hughes's literary output stands as an important counternarrative to newspaper reports of lynching. In fact, Hughes responded immediately to the lynching of Emmett Till with such a counternarrative when he wrote "Mississippi." With the deaths of Green and Lang still on his mind, Hughes's revisions of this poem reveal that he veered away from memorializing Till as an individual to attract attention and offer respect to the numerous other unnamed lynch victims who met their deaths in Mississippi.

The conclusion revisits the absence or inclusion of what I have identified as Hughes's seven major lynching poems in his final publication, *The Panther and the Lash* (1967). While red-baiting led to Hughes being unable to publish his antilynching poems in his earlier mainstream publications such as his *Selected Poems* and *The Langston Hughes Reader* during the 1950s, *The Panther and the Lash* marked a rare opportunity in Hughes's career in which he experienced relative artistic freedom. With such freedom, poems that Hughes had earlier worked so hard to pass were now unnecessary. Moreover, four of Hughes's most potent statements about lynching take on additional depth in this context as they further highlight issues addressed throughout this study.

Like no other writer, Langston Hughes offers a startling look at the surprisingly persistent and ever-changing aspects of American lynching culture. His poems, and the culture they portray, demonstrate how one African American artist negotiated various political shifts. For readers, this negotiation is an important reminder of the relevance of art as a response to a culture that invented new ways to defer delivering on its promises of equality, free speech, integration, and social justice.

> I heard the singing of the Mississippi when Abe Lincoln
> went down to New Orleans, and I've seen its muddy
> bosom turn all golden in the sunset.
>
> *Langston Hughes, "The Negro Speaks of Rivers"*

The Red Summer of 1919

Finding Reassurance

Langston Hughes appeared before Senator Joseph McCarthy and the House Committee on Un-American Activities on Thursday, March 26, 1953, in Washington, D.C. Hughes was called to testify under the guise of establishing whether or not federal funding should continue to be used to pay for placing his poetry overseas as part of a government program that promoted American ideals. The committee raised issues regarding whether or not Hughes's poems portrayed America to the rest of the world in a positive way the government could approve or whether they "strike a Communist, rather than an anti-Communist note" (United States 975). As the record shows, this was clearly not the motivation for this interrogation. In fact, Senator Joseph McCarthy himself asserted that neither of the poems about which Hughes was questioned throughout the testimony, "Goodbye Christ" or "One More 'S' in the USA" was "in any of the books in the collection in the information centers" (United States 986). As such, the true purpose of this hearing was to intimidate Hughes and others who dared to question the accepted expression of U.S. nationalism.

This public interrogation took place in Washington, D.C., near the banks of the Potomac River. Ninety-six years earlier, Langston's grandfather Lewis Leary was killed fighting with John Brown at the confluence of the Potomac and Shenandoah rivers. For Hughes, it may have felt as if history were circling upon itself rather than moving progressively forward.

Hughes's first published poem offers an opportunity to examine the role that rivers played in shaping Hughes's historical imagination. This poem also serves as an early statement of personal reassurance. This chapter focuses on "The Negro Speaks of Rivers," Hughes's first record of personal resistance against the threats of lynching.

▶•◀

While American riverscapes are considered the domain of white male heterosexuals and certainly had this reputation during his lifetime, Hughes found a way to unsettle this domination through an epiphany during his journey in a racially segregated Jim Crow train car that took him across the Mississippi River when he was eighteen. Hughes was on his way to visit his father, who was in Mexico after having emigrated there and become wealthy in the relative absence of racial barriers. While sitting in this confined space on account of his race, Hughes's train approached Missouri, the state in which he was born. Hughes began thinking about his father's hatred of African Americans, but he was also traveling closer and closer to the South with each passing minute. The South was home to millions of African American sharecroppers who remained in conditions little different than slavery. They lived in an environment that offered inhumane work, legal confinement, and the torture and death associated with lynchings.

Hughes had passed through Texas on this same route the year before during the Red Summer of 1919. Black soldiers returning from World War I in 1919 were confused about their lack of status, which prompted W.E.B. Du Bois to write: "We return. / We return from fighting. / We return fighting" (qtd. in Shapiro 157). Lynchings were at a high "approaching that of the 1890s," and Texas was one of the worst offenders (Lewis, *When Harlem Was in Vogue* 18). Everything had changed after the Red Summer of 1919: "There was something new to be seen in the rapid spread of violence, and within the various incidents there was also a component of more determined and effective black resistance to assault by white racists" (Shapiro 149–50).

Hughes faced a legitimate need to prepare himself for resistance as he approached Texas on this trip. The result was "The Negro Speaks of Rivers," which until now has not been read as an antilynching poem. We must remember that Hughes never lived outside a context where lynching existed in America, as the last official lynching was recorded in 1968, a year after his death. Having lived under the shadow of an attempted lynching in Lincoln, Illinois, in 1915, having heard published and unpublished stories regarding white-on-black violence all his life, and being faced with the prospect of traveling by train through Texas, Hughes clearly engages a fearsome landscape in 1920. By claiming intimacy with the world's historical rivers, however, he lessens his own fearfulness. To understand "The Negro Speaks of Rivers," we must read it as a statement of personal resistance given the context of American lynching culture. It is one example of the kind of art that comes forth when a human being is forced to live in the shadow of traumatizing dismemberment.

▶◀

Because the train ride took him near his birthplace of Joplin, Missouri, Hughes likely would have been reminded of his mother, who was essentially reduced to being a migrant worker who sought work from city to city. Even more important, empowering and comforting images of his grandmother Mary Langston, with whom he had lived for most of his childhood, also could have surfaced like the memories captured in his poetry.

In "Fulfillment" (1947), Hughes recalls nature being as open to him as it was to Walt Whitman. As a European American, Whitman not only appears to move freely throughout nature in his poetry, but he even imagines "Others" moving easily across the Brooklyn River as many as "Fifty" or "A hundred years hence" in his poem "Crossing Brooklyn Ferry" (lines 13–18). Whitman imagines these others "Will enjoy the sunset, the pouring-in of the flood-tide, the falling back to the sea of the ebb-tide" (19). Hughes's poetry reminds us that such enjoyment is not so easily available to all citizens. It is also important to note that Whitman was one of Hughes's favorite poets. In fact, while sailing to Africa in June 1922, Hughes dropped overboard all but one of the books he owned. The book he saved was Whitman's *Leaves of Grass*. He later stated: "I had no intention of throwing that one away" (Rampersad 1: 72).

In "Fulfillment," Hughes imagines what appear to be the naïve experiences of a child not yet conscious of the racism awaiting him. In the poem, the speaker imagines going to a river where he can touch "silver water" (6). While there, he imagines playing with sunlight as if it were a ball and sleeping through the night after the moonlight offers its blessing. This moonlight is compared to the good-night kiss of a "grand-mother" (17). The poem reminds both reader and writer that riverscapes can be sites of enjoyment for an African American. When the context of the past is not being invoked, the world of dreams sometimes offers Hughes a chance to imagine being satisfied in nature. Such dreaming reminds us that the reality is otherwise and that there is some deep desire to see the natural realm as a place to wander, dance, and whirl. Because the present reality forbids such an intimate relationship with rivers, Hughes sometimes locates his moments of place affection for these rivers in either the idealized past or the hoped-for future.

Growing up under the care of Mary Langston, Hughes had a clear awareness of his birthright to this dream of freedom. Her husband, Lewis Sheridan Leary, who had died fighting with John Brown at Harpers Ferry, was twenty-four years old when he fell to his death by gunfire when trying to cross the Shenandoah River. His "blood-stained, bullet riddled shawl" was brought home to Hughes's grandmother, who wore it as many as fifty years after his death and also used it to cover Hughes himself when he slept (Rampersad 1: 6). Hughes's "October 16: The Raid" (1931) establishes the confluence of the Shenandoah and Potomac rivers as its context. After reminding readers of the date of the attack on Harpers Ferry in 1859 with the title, Hughes emphasizes a historical version of remembering John Brown. Rather than a personal recollection or individual sentimentality, the reader is implored to revisit death, pain, and history at the significant national site.

The movement of this poem reminds us of how time and place are interrelated. The poem begins by emphasizing time in the title, moves on to the central person described overtly in the poem, recounts the events, then brackets John Brown and the raid within the construction of this chronotope "Where two rivers meet" (9). As such, this riverscape is the first context toward understanding the connections between these people and the events themselves.

Moreover, Hughes's own life becomes important evidence for uncovering why Hughes cares about remembering these events. One of the "twenty-one companions" (6) mentioned in the poem was his grandfather, Lewis Sheridan Leary. The eight-year-old Langston Hughes was with Mary Langston on August 31, 1910, in Osawatomie, Kansas, when the John Brown Memorial Battlefield was dedicated. The event must have had an overwhelming effect on Hughes, for he saw his grand-mother seated in a distinguished place of honor at the platform on a day when President Theodore Roosevelt delivered a speech calling for "New Nationalism" (Rampersad 1: 13). Hughes might also have re-membered a phrase he uses in the poem which both his grandmother and marchers in the Civil War used. The common phrase "his Soul is marching on" was used in reference to John Brown throughout Civil War marching songs and in Mary Langston's constant references to him (Rampersad 1: 6).

Hughes concludes the poem by alluding to the powerful imagery of Brown's death in a way that reminds readers of how these actions are connected to the place where two rivers meet. Here, Hughes assigns memory to a place rather than a people. He suggests that people forget what places will always remember. By documenting the knowledge of this placial history, Hughes also calls for the spirits of the men to return, suggesting that their work is still not done. As such, the poem does more than address a past history; it also draws attention to a familiar and ever-present need. Of course, it is the final plural s of "ghosts" (26) and "raiders" (27) that suggests Hughes's memory of Lewis Leary's fatal blow near the banks of the Shenandoah River. The actions of Brown and his band have forever changed the significance of this place. These men are the ones Mary Langston and Hughes remembered each time they warmed themselves with Lewis Leary's shawl.

►•◄

Mary Langston was denied a job as a teacher in the South and "turned down an invitation from the government of Haiti to live there as an honored guest" before marrying Charles Howard Langston (Ramper-sad 1: 6). After living for ten years as a widow following Lewis Leary's death, Mary Langston married Ralph Quarles, the son of a white Vir-ginia landowner. Quarles was wealthy and defiant, choosing to live with a former black slave "like man and wife" and allowing their children to inherit his land and estate (1: 6). Charles's younger brother John Mercer Langston, regarded as "one of the three best known black Americans of the nineteenth century," served as president of Howard University and Virginia College before being elected to Congress in 1890 (1: 7). Arnold Rampersad notes in regard to Hughes's distinguished relatives that he "nursed a sense that he was obliged within his lifetime, in some way, to match their deeds" (1: 18).

As the train carrying Hughes sped across the important riverscape of the Mississippi, we can imagine Hughes thinking of the various genealogy lines or tributaries running through his own self like a river. Rivers had always been important to Hughes, and he even attempted to publish three stories—"Eyes Like a Gypsy's," "Hello Henry," and "Posthumous Tale"—under the pseudonym "David Boatman" (Berry 220). The name "perhaps had deep symbolic meaning for Hughes—the black bard of rivers" (221). Such memories could have turned his momentary topophobic anxiety toward feelings of topophilia, feelings that remain intermingled within the poem. The larger cosmic rivers of the race become connected to the personal issues of race as Hughes takes his first step toward writing his way into his family's legacy with his first published poem, "The Negro Speaks of Rivers" (1921).

In writing "The Negro Speaks of Rivers," Hughes contemplated his future occupation as writer as well as the upcoming reunion with his father, who had moved to Mexico years earlier. Later he would recall: "All day on the train I had been thinking about my father, and his strange dislike of his own people. I didn't understand it, because I was Negro, and I liked Negroes very much" (qtd. in Smith 50). Hughes "brooded on his father's hatred of blacks" before writing this poem on the back of an envelope over the course of this train ride (Rampersad 1: 39). In effect, while imagining his father's abandonment of his African American heritage, Hughes found himself embracing his own.

Hughes had traveled with his father on this train trip to Mexico the year before. He specifically recalls his father's dislike of the poor blacks he saw on this trip: "The second day out from Cleveland, the train we were on rolled across Arkansas. As we passed through a dismal village in the cotton fields, my father peered from the window of our Pullman car at a cluster of black peons on the main street and said contemptuously: 'Look at the niggers'" (CW 13: 56). Hughes believed that his poems "generally" came from "something I'm thinking about," and Hughes's own comments about the thoughts that inspired this lyric point his reader's attention toward the two key places of St. Louis and Texas when he states that the poem was "written just outside St. Louis, as the train rolled toward Texas" (CW 13: 65). What is Hughes trying to tell us when he cites these two places as having a direct influence on this poem?

Interestingly enough, only pages earlier in his first autobiography,

The Big Sea, Hughes describes key experiences at each place. On the trip back to Cleveland in 1919, he willingly passed as a Mexican in San Antonio because "colored people had to use Jim Crow waiting rooms, and could not purchase a Pullman berth. There, I simply went in the main waiting room, as any Mexican would do, and made my sleeping car arrangements in Spanish" (*CW* 13: 62). As a result of arranging such accommodations, Hughes's identity was unveiled later that evening by a man "staring at him intently," who eventually shouted, "You're a nigger, ain't you?" (*CW* 13: 62).

Even later in the same trip, Hughes was denied service in St. Louis while waiting between trains. When asked by an attendant behind the counter if he was a Mexican or a Negro, Hughes replied: "'I'm colored.' . . . The clerk turned to wait on someone else" (*CW* 13: 63). By turning our attention to the fact that this poem was written a year later, "just outside of St. Louis" as the train approaches Texas, Hughes implies that this moment is filled with tension. We can imagine him steeling himself for tense encounters still to come.

In 1920, then, traveling alone to Mexico in the dangerous summer months when violence raged highest, Hughes negotiates traveling through Texas as follows: "At San Antonio he pulled his hat down over his curly hair and, in Spanish, secured a comfortable Pullman berth to Laredo" (Rampersad 1: 40). Hughes carefully avoids more than Jim Crow waiting rooms: he is astutely avoiding any confrontation that might potentially threaten his life. Lest we see this choice as an exaggeration, it should be remembered that the sixteen-year-old Lige Daniels was lynched in Center, Texas, on August 3, 1920, only seventeen days after Hughes passed through this state. It is little surprise that in the fall of 1921, Hughes chose to avoid passing back through Texas altogether when he left Mexico. He secured a passage by ship back to New York to attend Columbia University (Rampersad 1: 49). His experience of these fears at such a young age offers one explanation for why Hughes defends the young Scottsboro Boys with such intensity throughout the 1930s and empathizes with the fourteen-year-old Emmett Till; and it suggests why he feels compelled to write "The Bitter River" in 1942 in response to the lynching of two fourteen-year-old boys.

Furthermore, Hughes consistently associated lynching with Texas. In the poem "Negro" (1922), Hughes writes: "They lynch me now in Texas" (16). It is important to reclaim the fact that Texas is the state Hughes names in his early associations with U.S. lynching culture.

Fig. 1.1. Lynching of Lige Daniels in Center, Texas, August 3, 1920. By permission of the Allen-Littlefield Collection.

The "Negro Speaks of Rivers" expresses a longing to recapture an intimate relationship with riverscapes at a moment when Hughes is most fearful of the violence that could occur there. Hughes himself had heard numerous accounts of lynchings reported in the *Chicago Defender* while growing up in Lawrence, Kansas (Rampersad 1: 19). Lincoln, Illinois, had also been the scene of an attempted lynching when "hundreds of whites [tried] to seize an alleged black murderer from his jail" while Hughes was living there (Rampersad 1: 23). Hughes's birthplace of Joplin, Missouri, had also experienced a lynching soon after Hughes's birth:

> In April, 1903, a white mob stormed the city jail and lynched a black man arrested for the murder of a white policeman. Attacking the Bottoms, the mob burned houses indiscriminately. The next day, hundreds of blacks thronged the railway station. . . ."[S]ome of them never came back to the city," a local white historian reported, "and some others, feeling that the event had been a great humiliation to their race, moved away." (Rampersad 1: 11)

It is likely that Hughes's mother, Carrie, spoke to him about this event later in his life, and it is possible that these events had a direct effect on Hughes's father, who moved away from the United States for good at about this same time.

Hughes was thinking of his father as he traveled alone through Texas toward Mexico in 1920, and it is hard to overestimate just how intimidating the prospect of such a passage would be for an eighteen-year-old African American. The lynching of Henry Smith in Paris, Texas, in 1893 has been called "the inaugural example of lynching-as-mass-spectacle" (Gussow 29). This lynching was recorded in photographs, and a horrific sound recording of Smith's death by burning was made, sold, and exhibited for citizens to experience in places as far away as Seattle, Washington (Goldsby 13). Ted Smith had been burned alive in the streets of Greenville, Texas, on July 28, 1908; Allan Brooks had been lynched from an archway in downtown Dallas on March 3, 1910; and another unidentified African American was burned to death in August 1910. That the last of these men went unnamed in the photograph of his lynching is yet another reminder of his dehumanization. These are only a few of the known lynchings during this period. In fact, at least 492 people were lynched in Texas between 1882 and 1930.[1] Racial tension continued to rise in Texas during this period. In 1915, the Texas branch of the NAACP was formed. Not so coincidentally, the Ku Klux Klan was revived this

Fig. 1.2. Lynching of Jesse Washington in Waco, Texas, May 15, 1916. By permission of the Allen-Littlefield Collection.

same year. By 1919, the Texas branch of the NAACP led the nation with 7,046 official members.[2]

Brazos County, Texas, was one of the most fearsome places in the world. Cynthia Nevels has argued that "European immigrants of different nationalities—first Italian, then Irish, and finally Bohemian, or Czech—played crucial roles" in making Texas "the most multiethnic of southern states" (1–4). As these immigrants sought to claim the racial category of whiteness, "They did so by taking advantage of, or even participating in, the South's most brutal form of racial domination: the lynching of black men. . . . [T]he deaths of black men helped to resolve the immigrant's ambiguous racial identity and to bestow the privilege of whiteness" (Nevels 7). This status resulted in membership in a racial category that afforded such immigrants greater access to capital and justice (Nevels 8).

More significant for instilling appropriate caution in the young Hughes was the well-documented and highly publicized lynching of the illiterate seventeen-year-old farmhand Jesse Washington on May 15, 1916. The image here may suggest how the act of lynching a black man sustains a degree of racial unity through the category of whiteness. As Nevels suggests, the spectators' varying ethnic diversity is momentarily unified in a powerful performance as participants including Czech, Irish, and Italian Americans veil their European heritage.

The citizens stand together as more equal than diverse when they contrast each other with Washington's black body; however, many of these immigrants had arrived in America much earlier. Moreover, many of them could have been of British, German, or French heritage. They had already achieved an American identity, suggesting that additional motives beyond the need for Americanization were also at work to produce this lynching. As we will see, lynching accomplished multiple purposes simultaneously. This simultaneity is important to note because it draws attention to how the cultural logic of lynching worked. Issues concerning race, sexuality, violence, intimidation, power, and class are some of the inflections that created, sustained, and reaffirmed many of the parameters of American culture. This lynching also reminds us that even those citizens who were not present or actively involved were greatly affected. Racial meanings were created and sustained during this event. As in so many previous lynchings, images of the burned body of Jesse Washington were turned into more than fifty thousand postcards. Even though such postcards at the turn of the century "sold for only pennies, the appetite for them was so voracious that retail sales reached the phenomenal amount of $50 million by 1909" (Snyder 164–65). It is hard to overestimate the cultural power of such practices for simultaneously legitimatizing lynching and terrorizing potential victims.

The lynching became so well known that it is often referred to as the "Waco horror." Immediately after his trial on May 15, Washington "was beaten and dragged to the suspension bridge spanning the Brazos River. . . . [Later] Washington was castrated, and his ears were cut off. A tree supported the iron chain that lifted him above the fire of boxes and sticks. Wailing, the boy attempted to climb the skillet-hot chain. For this the men cut off his fingers. The executioners repeatedly lowered the boy into the flames and hoisted him out again. With each repetition, a mighty shout was raised" (Allen 174). Waco's mayor, who "watched the entire episode from the second floor of City Hall, was concerned that the lynchers might damage the tree" (Bernstein 4). What was left of the body was lassoed to the back of a horse and pulled around town until Washington's skull "bounced loose"; then he was dragged behind a car before having what little remained of him hung from a telephone pole in a sack (Bernstein 111).

Washington was accused of "bludgeoning to death fifty-three-year-old Lucy Fryer, the wife of a white farmer in Robinson," and later "black journalist A. T. Smith, editor of the *Paul Quinn Weekly*, was arrested and convicted of criminal libel after he printed allegations that Lucy Fryer's husband had committed the murder."[3] Washington "signed a confession he could not read" with an *X* (Apel and Smith, *Lynching Photographs* 47). This "confession was published in all three Waco newspapers" (Apel and Smith, *Lynching Photographs* 47). Approximately fifteen thousand people attended the lynching.

It is important to note that bridges were often selected as sites for lynchings. Such visible landmarks intimidated African Americans and reinforced white superiority. Taking Washington's body to a bridge that spanned the Brazos River served as a visual reminder of who controls such nomadic space. It also turned this monumental space into a site for warped celebration.

The NAACP had intensified its formal campaign against U.S. lynching culture in 1919 with its publication of *Thirty Years of Lynching in the U.S. (1889–1918)*. The NAACP's rising presence in Texas culminated in a brutal beating during this year. When a white secretary for the organization appeared "in Texas to prevent his organization from being closed down by the state, [he] was beaten unconscious on a street in Austin" (Rampersad 1: 35). Also in the summer of 1919, the Longview Race Riot occurred in Longview, Texas, from July 10 to 18. After Samuel L. Jones and Calvin P. Davis urged local cotton pickers to refrain from selling to local white brokers, and the June 17 murder of Lemuel Walters was reported in the July 10 edition of the *Chicago Defender*, Jones was beaten and his house burned to the ground because whites assumed he had written the *Defender* article. Davis's house, other black homes, and a black dance hall were torched as well. Dr. Davis's father was also killed, and a total of eight Texas Rangers and 250 national guardsmen were called in to enforce martial law.[4] The *Defender* and *Crisis* covered this event in detail.

It is important to remember that "the nation's black press gave the events the most thorough coverage" (Apel and Smith, *Lynching Photographs* 49). Hughes would have read about these events in "detail in the Cleveland papers," and they "must have weighed heavily on Langston's mind. . . . At last he began to understand fully . . . that he was a black man in a nation hostile to all people of his race " (Rampersad 1: 35). Moreover, the NAACP worked hard to chronicle such injustices through its publication *Crisis*, and Hughes reminds us that he "grew up with the NAACP. . . . [and] learned to read with *The Crisis* on my Grandmother's lap" (*CW* 10: 197).

From the beginning of its existence in 1910, *Crisis* published running totals of the number of black lynching victims. Moreover, the second and third issues each included illustrations that addressed lynching. One showed a black youth hanging from a tree with fire and smoke billowing below his feet. Another full-page sketch titled *The National Pastime* portrayed a black woman's despair at finding that her loved one's lynching had made front-page headlines in the daily press. Coverage of lynchings was not reserved for illustrations or graphs. One of the earliest issues declared "there has not been a lynching in Great Britain with its 40,000,000 people, in over eighty years."[5]

While these stories informed Hughes's youth as he sat upon his grandmother's lap, headlines from *Crisis* increased in intensity in the years surrounding his first trip through Texas. The inside covers of consecutive issues of *Crisis* announced in bold letters "Help Crush out Lynching" and "Are *You* Going to Allow Lynching Mobs to Continue?"[6] The state of Texas was mentioned prominently. Advertisements for three leaflets written by John Shillady, James Weldon Johnson, and Mary White Ovington in response to the August 22, 1919, attack on an NAACP secretary in Austin were advertised on the inside cover of the October issue; the Houston branch of the NAACP reported a victim had been "buried secretly and no publicity given to the facts"; and the magazine reported the "indications of a revival of the Klan in Texas." Furthermore, the lynching report, once a small statistical graph, had now grown to a two-page record by February 1919 that included victims' names, and the dates and locations of their lynchings.[7]

More significantly, the July 1916 issue of *Crisis* ran an eight-page story on the lynching of Jesse Washington, which featured six photographs of Washington's burned body. It included descriptions of Washington having his fingers cut off and receiving twenty-five stab wounds until his "body was a solid color of red" ("The Waco Horror" 5). Much of African Americans' knowledge of lynchings came through newsprint articles and photography so that, in one regard, this brutality "remained paradoxically distant and perhaps fantastic" (Hale 204). At the same time, however, this subject was also intensely immediate and personal.

Moreover, the *Chicago Defender* ran stories about Jesse Washington's lynching on May 16, June 3, and June 10, 1916 (Bernstein 134).

Henry D. Middleton has reported that *Defender* editor J. Hockley Smiley sometimes published "exciting fabrications of crimes against blacks" (Bernstein 133). This sensationalizing, if not manufacturing, of stories reminds us that Hughes would have been exposed to the most dramatic (and sometimes invented) stories of lynchings. Access to these published stories made Texas one of the most intimidating places for an African American to travel through in 1920. All these events not only happened, but they were also documented and reported well enough for Hughes to be intimately aware of them.

Hughes's emotional response to the print media's accounts was overwhelming. Speaking to Chicago's Windy City Press Club in 1957, he spoke of his fears: "When I was a child, headlines in the colored papers used to scare the daylights out of me. I grew up in Kansas and for years I was afraid to go down South, thinking—as a result of the Negro press—that I might be lynched the minute I got off the train" (*CW* 9: 354). Earlier in his life, Hughes reflected back on what it was like traveling through the South in his younger years: "I rather expected to see a lynching every day" (*CW* 13: 217). Given his repeated testimony, it is hard to imagine Hughes being able to completely suppress these same fears while passing through the South on his first train trip alone.

As he penned the first line of his poem while on the train near St. Louis, Hughes quickly approached the place he was born, Joplin, Missouri. In approaching this place, stories of the man lynched shortly after his birth, its possible link to his father's decision to leave the United States, the fears of lynching first experienced in Kansas, and the reality that Jesse Washington was only one year younger than Hughes himself at the time he was lynched would have taken on greater significance. Hughes writes: "Now it was just sunset, and we crossed the Mississippi, slowly over a long bridge. I looked out the window of the Pullman at the great muddy river flowing down toward the heart of the South, and I began to think what that river, the old Mississippi, had meant to Negroes in the past—how to be sold down the river was the worst fate that could overtake a slave in times of bondage. . . . Then I began to think about other rivers in our past—the Congo, and the Niger, and the Nile in Africa" (*CW* 13: 65–66). Hughes may also have been remembering what the Mississippi River meant in 1920 as well as what it meant in the distant past. Among other things, when a race war exploded in Philips County, Arkansas, from October 1 to 3, 1919, only twenty-five blacks were officially listed as dead. However, "Many blacks believed that perhaps as many as 200 were killed, their bodies dumped in the Mississippi River." Likewise, official records of an earlier massacre in Wilmington, North Carolina, originally claimed that as few as ten people died although others "may have been buried in unmarked mass graves" (Smith McKoy 48). It also appears that "hundreds more may have been killed, their bodies dumped into the [Cape Fear] River."[8]

It is these events and other culturally significant stories Hughes references when he begins "The Negro Speaks of Rivers" by writing: "I've known rivers" (1). The speaker soon remembers even more after initially calling upon the adolescent joys and pleasures of an idealized past. He continues to establish a tone of remembrance and affection throughout the next five lines of the poem:

> I've known rivers ancient as the world and older than the flow
> of human blood in human veins.
>
> My soul has grown deep like the rivers.
>
> I bathed in the Euphrates when dawns were young.
> I built my hut near the Congo and it lulled me to sleep.
> I looked upon the Nile and raised the pyramids above it. (2–7)

In the crisis of developing and enunciating his important subject position, Hughes chooses the stories and endurance of his grandmother Mary Langston over the flight and forgetfulness of his angry father, Jim Hughes. Rampersad wisely notes that Hughes is "clinging to his greatest faith, which is his people and his sense of kinship with them" (1: 40). However, it is also "a majestic reminder of the strength and fullness of history, of the sources of that life which transcends even ceaseless labor and burning crosses" (Jemie 140). The poem opens up even further when set against the context of how Hughes and other African Americans were engaging with riverscapes.

In telling readers that he has known rivers, Hughes also revealed a great many other things about his memory. First, he demonstrated that one of the reasons his memory was so strong at this time was because of a desire to actively engage with nature. In fact, our memories are most powerful toward a given subject when our literal engagement with that subject is lowest.[9] Second, as the poem unfolds, the phrase "I've known rivers" becomes synonymous with "I know history." The history that Hughes knows is twofold in that he understands his personal history and the call to be a representative of the people for whom Lewis Leary fought and died at Harpers Ferry. Yet he also embraces a collective history that overleaps time to recall that "I have bathed in the Euphrates when dawns were young, / I built my hut near the Congo and it lulled me to sleep" (5–6).

Third and finally, Hughes remembers the affection for places such as the Euphrates and the Congo as he also suggests the anxiety or fear that accompanies such places. Experiencing topophobia, Hughes relives the pain of slavery and the pleasure of being a representative for a people when he writes, "I looked upon the Nile and raised the pyramids above it" (7). It is precisely the complex relationship between affection and anxiety over riverplaces with which Hughes himself is grappling. Equally important, these two emotions are precisely what need to be sifted and considered carefully in Hughes's poem.

Hughes references the brutalities of the Congo in a poem written at the same time as "The Negro Speaks of Rivers." In "The Negro" (1922), Hughes writes that "The Belgians cut off my hands in the Congo" (15). Hughes seeks the comforts of the Congo, which can stand in place of King Leopold's edict that the people pay a 10 percent labor tax. From 1885 to 1908, soldiers "were required to produce the right hand of villagers who had been executed for not paying the tax" (Babb 55). Removing the right hand eventually became punishment enough, "leaving thousands of maimed victims" (55).

Furthermore, following the ideas of Hortense Spillers, enslaving the human bodies of females became reduced to a metaphor for "*externalized* acts of torture and prostration that we imagine as the peculiar province of *male* brutality and torture" (59). She continues: "This profitable 'atomizing' of the captive body provides another angle on the divided flesh: we lose any hint or suggestion of a dimension of ethics, of relatedness between human personality and its anatomical features, between one human personality and another, between human personality and cultural institutions. To that extent, the procedures adopted for the captive flesh demarcate a total objectification, as the entire captive community becomes a living laboratory" (60). For Spillers, this "atomizing" results in a new definition of "value" (60), as the body becomes an object that can be used without its consumer falling prey to any ethical scrutiny. Within the circling aspect of what Hughes feels in regards to American lynching culture, this brutality has again proven to be cyclic rather than progressive.

Building upon Spillers's ideas, one way for the male human bodies of African American lynch victims to achieve commodity value rests in their ability to intimidate and instill fear among the living. The body parts taken as souvenirs are powerful remainders. They signal the uninitiated as they perform their own important work of forever reclaiming the pain exacted on the victim. Such souvenirs give the multiethnic owner a deeper claim to the unifying category of whiteness; even after the spectacle is over, those who posses such artifacts gain even further status by holding the narrative authority to document and retell details about the event to future listeners. More significantly, lynching souvenirs also remind their viewers that the victim's pain and the mob's work can be restaged again in reaction to any incident.

Hughes attempts to reclaim the beauty of the Congo in the face of his knowledge of its dehumanizing brutality. Near the end of the poem, Hughes writes himself into the final history of the Mississippi: "I heard the singing of the Mississippi when Abe Lincoln / went down to New Orleans and I've seen its muddy / bosom turn all golden in the sunset" (8–10). By doing so, he is going beyond reasserting his connection with his African American heritage to reclaim a sense of selfhood that stands in sharp contrast to that of his father. This newfound sense of selfhood will allow him to speak as the black bard of rivers. As such, he charts this historical geography of riverscapes in ways that recount past atrocities such as lynching. He reveals that the human damage done to African Americans has been pushed aside at a time when the nation is beginning to plan systems of river dams and focus on water rights at precisely the same sites where African American bodies are being treated as waste to be dumped in the night—rivers are being regarded as acceptable sites for mass graves. In addition, African American anxiety surrounding Hughes's use of the word "Mississippi" in this poem should not be overlooked. Jazzman Danny Barker recalled the connotations the word carried in the 1920s: "Just the mention of the word Mississippi . . . would cause complete silence and attention. The word was so powerful that it carried the impact of catastrophes, destruction, death, hell, earthquakes, cyclones, murder, hanging, lynching, all sorts of slaughter" (qtd. in Gussow 32).

Why might Hughes reference Lincoln in this poem? The reference to Abraham Lincoln's trip to New Orleans has at least four important connections to Hughes's own personal journey. First, like Hughes himself, Lincoln was in his late teens (nineteen) when he made his "first trip upon a flat-boat to New-Orleans" (Zall 16). Second, Lincoln also "entered the Mississippi where it made a great bend above St. Louis" (Keneally 14). Third, this trip was the first time each of these men gained firsthand experience of the brutal conditions experienced by blacks. John Hanks suggests how moved Lincoln was by what he saw when he first went to New Orleans: "There it was when we saw Negroes chained, maltreated, whipped, and scourged. Lincoln saw it; his heart bled, said nothing much. . . . I can say, knowing it, that it was on this trip that he formed his opinions of slavery. It ran its irons in him then and there" (Keneally 14–15). Fourth and finally, Lincoln was exposed to a fearful encounter when his "raft was attacked at night by a group of seven slaves armed with knives" (Keneally 11). This encounter was so tenuous that Lincoln "was nearly killed by a group of runaway slaves who attempted to rob his party as they traveled down the river" (Pinsker 12).

Like Lincoln, Hughes faced all these concerns in varying degrees on his trip. In regard to Lincoln, "Many would speculate later on what would have befallen America if the ultimate Great Emancipator had been killed on the Mississippi in 1828 by those he would later free" (Keneally 11). In regard to Hughes, one wonders who would have provided adequate rhetoric and sufficient poetic metaphors to counter American lynching culture if he had met the same fate as Lige Daniels.

Hughes's use of "sunset" in "The Negro Speaks of Rivers" is also highly significant. First, it takes us back to the quote by Hughes in his autobiography in which he states: "Now it was just sunset, and we crossed the Mississippi, slowly, over a long bridge" (CW 13: 65). Hughes's image of a "bridge" is a personal memory intensifier reminding us that he is passing into the South on the type of structure often used to attach lynching ropes to victim's necks. Second, Hughes's personal enjoyment of this particular sunset is a poignant statement of resistance to the terror of lynching culture. Signs bearing the statement "Nigger, don't let the sun set on you here" were well known to many citizens who lived in the segregation-era South. In fact, Hughes even directly references his knowledge of such signs in his autobiography The Big Sea (13: 217). Hughes chooses to bask in confidence and defiance as the sun sets on a riverscape that lynching culture has tried to use for purposes of torture and intimidation. The description of its "muddy bosom" is itself a reminder of the black bodies that have been dumped in such rivers. These darkened bodies, spoken of only in hushed tones, "turn all golden" as Hughes acknowledges the dead and refuses to let the natural wonders of this riverscape be ruined. Readers may also think of "The Trumpet Player" (1949), in which hardship somehow "Mellows to a golden note" (44). The violent memories of the past are somehow channeled by the creative process to form memorable art that allows the musician and poet to continue on in apparent ease. The poem displays Hughes's talent for discreetly addressing and veiling its undercurrent of lynching at a time when such discretion was an effective means of coded resistance.

Hughes's reference to "sunset" suggests that he has enjoyed the pleasures of this riverscape by daylight rather than in the nighttime. Throughout his poetry, river imagery and star imagery are intermingled, not exclusive. In "Ballad of the Seven Songs" (1949), Hughes writes of freedom with imagery that invokes the images of river and stars. Hughes's speaker is a slave named "Cudjoe" who hopes that the "stars that guide lone sailing boats / Across the dark sea" will also "guide thou me!" (62–64). Frederick Douglass's paper the *North Star* is referenced throughout the rest of the poem as emancipation is celebrated "*on* the river" and "*Up* the river" (192–95, emphasis added) rather than *down* the river. The North Star that guided slaves to freedom becomes a "universal star" to other lands and peoples still desperate for their own degree of freedom. Invoked in too many places in Hughes's poetry to consider fully here, this North Star is also portrayed as a "Guiding star!" (9) in "Slave Song" (1949).

A brief survey of four other poems in which Hughes invokes the imagery of stars should suffice to conclude a discussion of the way in which he suggests the journey of freedom through the use of star imagery. The stars are another universal symbol for freedom in "America" (1925), where multiple seekers of freedom who have come from Africa and Europe are described as being part of an America that is "star-seeking" (10). The poem "Star Seeker" (1926) reminds readers that such desire can be painful, for the speaker tells us that seeking after a star's beauty can force others to "Now behold my scars" (10). The desire for freedom can result in violent beating. In "Lullaby" (1926), it is the image of stars (mentioned six times in twenty-five lines) that is recalled as something beautiful and memorable. The poem's dedication "to a black mother" links the soothing memory of freedom to the mother. Finally, "Stars" (1926) encourages a young black child who lives in Harlem to "Reach up" his hand and "take a star" (7).

Of what do Hughes's star images remind us? Like blues lyrics that transcode their anger against authority by making references to the men or women through the trope of love, stars serve a similar purpose. They can stand in as safe images because outside readers appreciate their beauty while insiders read them as a coded means to address the search for freedom. They also reclaim the historical fact that stars were used by runaway slaves as guides along their routes of escape. Unlike a pastoral tradition that might use star imagery to imagine some individual liberation on an imaginative level, the freedoms suggested, remembered, and relived in Hughes's poems are reminders of a collective and literal historic liberation.

In a surprising revelation, it is Hughes's poetry and such use of stars that demonstrate a much more complete, ecocentric view of the world than the pastoral poetry of the Romantics, for here the star is a reminder of the actual usefulness of stars. In Hughes's poetry, a star is remembered as an ally to freedom and prized for its authentic and intrinsic values as opposed to an image that can be emptied and refilled, resignified as an image of selfhood, imaginative discovery, and ultimately a vehicle for perpetuating a homocentric world view. It is Hughes's poetry that draws readers back to the very real usefulness and intimate encounters with stars and rivers, reminding us that the imagery and beauty of the night stars allow us to actively participate with an environment that is inexhaustibly linked with the activities of cultural and political history.

Just as Hughes recognizes that star dreams are the realm of his ancestors, he now calls upon a daytime reality in "The Negro Speaks of Rivers" to calm and reassure himself. Seeing the sunset is a means for measuring the longed-for and imagined linear progression from slavery, to emancipation, to sharecropping, to greater and greater freedom.

▶•◀

What happens when we forget to ask where Hughes is when he finds affection for rivers, describes past places, or makes a historical reference to Abraham Lincoln in "The Negro Speaks of Rivers"? First, we completely ignore Hughes's own passage across the Mississippi in favor of an archetypal discussion of other important rivers in the world. In addition, we overlook the context of key references: the references to Lincoln and past riverscapes serve as an essential part of Hughes's personal strategy for achieving meditative reassurance. If we are not attentive to these references, we read Hughes right out of his own poem. We would also miss the all-important fact that Hughes's affection for these rivers captures a hard-fought personal struggle to resist intimidation.

Unlike those individuals who have easy access to nature, Hughes can enjoy this riverscape only after determinedly addressing his fears of facing injustice. In so doing, he may actually achieve an even deeper sense of topophilia as a result of having overcome these fears. To grasp the intensity of this affection, we must keep Hughes's placedness in mind when reading this poem. A historical context in itself will not do; we must also be placewise.

What kind of art results when a human being is forced to live in the shadow of such traumatizing dismemberment? Albert Murray states in *Stomping the Blues* that "what is ultimately at stake is morale, which is to say the will to persevere, the disposition to persist and perhaps prevail, and what must be avoided by all means is a failure of nerve" (10). In many ways, the poem becomes a meditative lyric that contemplates the ways in which African Americans have previously survived and flourished near riverscapes. The meditation implies that because others have survived, Hughes and his readers can survive, too. The poem serves as a record of how Hughes calmed his nerves by reminding himself of this fact despite facing racism. Reassurance is one of the many modes that counters the forces that would extinguish the right to life. Filled with uncommon dignity, it offers a counterattack to the intimidation associated with spectacle lynching. Hughes must have attached much personal significance to a poem that serves as a reminder that passing through the South can be a survivable act. Historical and personal memories are essential to overcoming the psychological trauma of imagining one's body become the subject of sadistic souveniring.

Having claimed his rightful place in his rich genealogy, Hughes moves from calming himself to asserting himself in the all-important last line of the poem. He has drawn all the places, people, and experiences into the deepest core of his body, and he concludes: "I've known rivers: / Ancient, dusky rivers. / My soul has grown deep like the rivers" (11–13). John Brown's soul is marching on deep within Hughes. Hughes had certainly "known" that Lincoln had formed his early opinions about slavery near the Mississippi on a trip to New Orleans, but in actually seeing this riverscape for himself he also learned more about the contemporary equivalents to slavery. These final lines are the equivalent of saying, "I've known the stories surrounding my relatives; now their burdens have become my passion." Spectacle lynching and sharecropping demanded another call for freedom, resistance, and assertion. The poem's last lines also reveal Hughes's intimate sense of awe and affection for rivers. Having personally faced and overcome his fears, his growing topophilia for such places achieves its greatest depth when Hughes suggests that the truest tenor for himself comes when he locates his identity through the vehicle of a river. Identity itself has been shaped and hardened through the coalescence of this process of writing while traveling through nomadic space. Hughes also hoped that, by showing and telling through future writings, the federal government and sympathetic audiences might break this cyclic pattern and truly advance justice.

With this poem, Hughes discovered not only the poetic voice that would mark his career, but also a way for others to celebrate African American culture. This poem became the signature poem of the Harlem Renaissance, in which African Americans sought to engage a broad public audience in African American culture and the difficulties accompanying its production through various artistic works. The poem has been set to music by the African American pianist and composer Margaret Bonds and sung by Marian Anderson when she appeared with the Chicago Symphony, printed on postcards and sent out to 250 friends of the *Crisis* in 1941, and used as the basis for a film proposal Hughes pushed in Hollywood.[10] The Harlem Renaissance proved to be a turning point for African Americans, in which pride in themselves and their race led to their seeking a greater place in American public life. The nation itself became more aware of its problems, and some worked publicly to change things. Eventually, such changes led to the civil rights movement and the overthrow of legally sanctioned segregation, changes that gave African Americans some opportunity to move more freely in the environment and to begin to pursue what it could offer them in pleasure and enjoyment.

Many African Americans knew "The Negro Speaks of Rivers" by heart. As I have discussed elsewhere, Evelyn White recited it from memory to calm her own fears of experiencing racial violence in 1995 when she went rafting down the McKenzie River in Oregon during a writing conference (33). In fact, at Hughes's funeral, only minutes before his body was to be cremated, a group of mourners gathered around: "they joined hands, bowed their heads, and recited the words of 'The Negro Speaks of Rivers.' Then they watched as attendants rolled away the body, toward the flames" (Rampersad 2: 425). Intimately connected with the prospect of death and the countless victims of the Red Summer of 1919, "The Negro Speaks of Rivers" has created a vision for reclaiming beauty by overcoming the dangers associated with American riverscapes.

This experience for the youthful Hughes also helped to shape his life-long empathy for young black male lynch victims such as the Scottsboro Boys, Ernest Green, Charlie Lang, and Emmett Till. With each rereading of the poem, we can imagine Hughes, the black bard of rivers, poising himself with much-needed reassurance, filling with racial pride, and turning painful and silenced violence into a growing (spoken) strength. His phrase "I've known rivers" comes to consciousness while he thinks of his esteemed relatives as the train keeps moving, always moving closer to Texas.

Bitter bearer of burdens
And singer of weary song,
I've drunk at the bitter river
With its filth and its mud too long.

Langston Hughes, "The Bitter River"

2

The Scottsboro Case and World War II America

Poetic Anger

There are striking overtones suggested by the images found in the original lithograph for the cover of Hughes's 1932 edition of *Scottsboro Limited*. It is important to consider the images that accompany Hughes's works carefully because they appear so frequently. In fact, more of Hughes's poems have been accompanied by graphic art than have the poems of any other poet in the twentieth century (Axelrod, Roman, and Travisano 694). In the lithograph, six figures in black outline all look to their left; they are black silhouettes whose individual features are not visible. The artist intended this anonymity, I suppose. Two hands reach up as if to ask "why?" But these hands are only the secondary images one notices when studying this cover. The first image, clearly positioned in the center and upper third of the cover, is a detailed rendering of a telegraph pole. There are two other poles as well, one off to the left, whose upper cross-arms are set somewhere outside the frame of the image itself.

Fig. 2.1. Cover of *Scottsboro Limited* (1932). By permission of Fordham University Press.

The third and final pole is set in the lower right corner as if it were in some distant past or distant future. But the pole in the center is something like a present moment, and its wires extend down toward the throats of the six shapeless victims below. There are nine wires here, and the message is clear. These wires are not wires any more than the telegraph posts are poles. These wires intersect with the poles to form nine lynching ropes. Three of the ropes extend to three figures huddled in a great indistinguishable mass. This lithograph emphasizes how the arrest of nine black youths in Scottsboro, Alabama, in 1931 evoked overtones of lynching. None of the Scottsboro Boys were the victims of a literal lynching.

Interestingly enough, this cover image was the third version completed by Prentiss Taylor.[1] Taylor initiated the painstaking process of completing these lithographs after he read Hughes's play *Scottsboro Limited*. Each of these three images offers slight revisions. Taylor's first attempt at illustrating these young men portrays them in the work clothes each was wearing at the time of their arrest; the second version, published in the December 1932 issue of *Crisis*, has the figures adorned in prison robes with noticeably whitened eyes to capture their fright. The final cover image, included here, was completed six months later without the white eyes and with the addition of a formal jacket and tie for one of the figures. Taylor himself wrote to Hughes about what he had hoped to accomplish: "it is supposed to convey an almost complete passivity . . . waiting for the thing that is going to happen to them—and there above their heads all the telephone wires like a gallows. . . . I try (however vaguely) to encompass the three tenses—it all goes in with some ideas I have about time that are too much to set down now" (Kellner 13). Given Taylor's gesture toward time, the boxcar on which the men are sitting becomes symbolic of the place in which the crime supposedly happened. The final clothing choices suggest the work overalls worn by the youths at the time of the arrest, the prison clothes donned later in jail, and the ties and coats eventually worn when they appeared in court. The future hanging of the men is suggested with the gallows imagery, as well as with the near lynchings that both preceded and remained an ever-present danger throughout the trial.

The infamous events in Scottsboro, Alabama, intensified Hughes's poetic campaign against lynching. On March 25, 1931, nine young black men were arrested in Scottsboro and charged with raping two white women named Victoria Price and Ruby Bates. Price's past criminal offenses, which included misdemeanor convictions for fornication and adultery that resulted in her serving time in jail, were regarded as inadmissible evidence in the trials. The original trials surrounding these men were a judicial farce. In the first hearing, eight of the men were sentenced to death. After no fewer than five appeals to other courts, including the U.S. Supreme Court in November 1932, the men were not sent to the electric chair. These men spent at least six and a half years in prison for a crime they clearly did not commit. Two men spent more than seventeen years in jail.

Evidence that suggests these two women lied includes, but is not limited to, the fact that Dr. R. R. Bridges's examination of Victoria Price noted the lack of bruises, cuts, or a significant amount of semen in the cervix of a woman who alleged that she had been raped by six men on the rough quartz and gravel floor of a train car (Geis and Bienen 60). Eventually a letter penned by Bates herself surfaced in which she stated that "those policeman made me tell a lie. . . . [T]hose Negroes did not touch me. . . . [I] wish those Negroes are not Burnt on account of me" (Cunard 273). Nancy Cunard's report on the second trial of Heywood Patterson finds that Bates eventually testified in the second hearing that she had "not even known the meaning of the word 'rape'" (279). Despite this testimony from one of the supposed victims of this crime, Patterson was found guilty. Bates's appearance on Mother's Day, May 14, 1934, in Washington D.C. (where she was accompanied by five of the mothers of the Scottsboro Boys) was an attempt to earn a presidential appeal for these young men.[2] Corruption clearly surrounded these trials.

Melvin B. Tolson remembers that Hughes was immediately moved by these events. In New York when he heard the news, Hughes drove hurriedly to attend a public meeting about the case: "There is a tenseness, an agony in the Poet's face. It seems that his life depends on getting to that meeting in time. . . . The Poet talks passionately of the Scottsboro boys. They are innocent. They must go free" (qtd. in Rampersad 1: 216–17). It is hard to overestimate just how important this case was to Hughes. As Hughes himself would remark in 1933: "The time has passed . . . for us to sit by and bemoan our fate. We need now an art and a literature which will arouse us to our fate. Already we have had too much literature in the vein of the spirituals, lamenting our fate and bemoaning our condition, but suggesting no remedy except humbleness and docility" (qtd. in Berry 183).

When Hughes read his poetry in 1931 in Ruby Bates's hometown of Huntsville, Alabama, he tried to interview her personally. Local teachers at Oakwood refused to help him locate her, and Hughes remembered them suggesting that "I would be taking my life in my hands" (CW 14: 90). While there, Hughes learned by word of mouth from the residents of Huntsville that Bates had let it be known in town that she had lied about being raped, saying that the "boys had not touched either her or Victoria Price" (CW 14: 90).

Energized by these visits, Hughes eventually invested a remarkable amount of time in the Scottsboro cause. In a letter written from Carmel, California, to Carl Van Vechten dated 1933 (a full two years after his initial visit to Kilby prison), Hughes mentions lynching and the case at the same time:

> You'll probably be getting an official letter from me and the Scottsboro committee out here shortly. We're writing all those who've been swell about Negroes in their creative work, and who we hope will help us help those black kids who are living in a state of terror now in their cells in Birmingham. (The lynch temper is growing everywhere. You probably read about those Mexican cotton pickers shot to death out here.) At Carmel we're planning a series of concerts and lectures for Scottsboro Funds to start this month, and a sale of original manuscripts of Negro and White writers. (*Remember Me to Harlem* 110)

Writing so that "lynch laws might not triumph," Hughes's letters asked recipients for financial assistance and a brief statement to be used for immediate press release.[3] In February 1934, no fewer than thirty-five months after news of the case first broke, Hughes was still concentrating his efforts on the Scottsboro case. He writes to Van Vechten: "[H]ave I written you this month, I have been so busy, what with books and Scottsboro and all? . . . [S]he [Mary Van Vechten Blanchard] sent us a check for Scottsboro. . . . Some swell manuscripts from England have arrived for our Sale—Huxley, Swinnerton, Russell, Huddleston; and from New York, a marvelous Steichen print, four Lynn Wards and two Julius Blockes" (*Remember Me to Harlem* 118).

Hughes's investment in raising funds appeared to have been satisfying and successful:

> Ella Winter, her friend, Marie Short, and I, with some other Carmel writers and artists, organized a big Scottsboro auction of original paintings and drawings which many of America's leading artists contributed. We had intended to hold the auction at Carmel, but so many pictures and sketches arrived in answer to our letters that we transferred the sale to San Francisco where, with James Cagney as auctioneer, a considerable sum was raised for the defense of the Scottsboro Boys. (*CW* 14: 280)

These efforts resulted in Hughes being able to report small triumphs in winning the nation's attention to the incidents in Alabama. He writes to Van Vechten, noting that: "Since our activities out here the California papers have at least begun to report news of the Scottsboro trials, and one of the big columnists has written about it twice. They didn't seem to have heard about it before, this far West" (*Remember Me to Harlem* 117). Finally, Hughes marks another small victory in his efforts to drawing national attention to this case. To capture the interrelatedness between this case and the subject of lynching, note the unedited sequence of Hughes's thinking in this letter to Van Vechten dated December 6, 1933:

> Swell of you to send that check for Scottsboro. Please accept through me the committee's official thanks for your generous support. Several checks and excellent statements have come in from my letters, particularly from the Southerners, Du Bois, Paul Green, and Blair Niles. You probably saw Fannie Hurst's fine letter in the New York papers. . . . Haven't been able to get any sort of response from Julia Peterkin, though. Or Roark Bradford. . . . Guess you heard about President Roosevelt denouncing lynching over the radio the other night. Well, we certainly stormed up a barrage of wires to him from out here, so maybe that helped some. Noel and some other members of our Committee were just about to go to Scottsboro when the trials were put off again. (*Remember Me to Harlem* 113)

The extent of just how far the news of Scottsboro spread in the 1930s is staggering. Hughes spent part of 1932 traveling in Russia with a film group. Faith Berry recounts that, "For Hughes, attending a Scottsboro rally in Moscow that July was nothing he would not have done in the United States, where his booklet *Scottsboro Limited* was being distributed in his absence. When offers came to translate it into Russian that summer, he requested that proceeds from sales be sent to the Scottsboro Defense Fund" (161). There were also formal protests in Britain and Berlin (Rice 15). One can only imagine the shock Hughes felt overseas in Russia when he received the following courtesy: "with the Scottsboro Case in worldwide trial in the papers everywhere, and especially in Russia, folks went out of their way to show us courtesy. On a crowded bus, nine times out of ten, some Russian would say, 'Negrochanski tovarish—Negro comrade—take my seat!'" (*CW* 14: 99).

When *Scottsboro Limited* was in the process of being published by Hughes in 1932, he wrote to Prentiss Taylor saying "I'm more excited about this Scottsboro booklet . . . than anything I've ever had published" (Rampersad 1: 235). Taylor did the four lithographs that appeared in the book, and upon final publication Hughes wired that it was the "MOST BEAUTIFUL BOOK I HAVE EVER SEEN" (Rampersad 1: 241). The booklet included four poems and a play on Scottsboro. One of the poems was simply titled "The Town of Scottsboro." Taylor's lithograph for this poem featured a courthouse hovering above a portrayal of a slave market. Most telling, a "cat-o'-nine-tails," commonly used to punish slaves, borders the image. In his poem, Hughes insists on personifying the place of Scottsboro in the first two lines, and in the third line, which collapses the distance between courtroom and mob: "No shame is writ across its face—/ Its court, too weak to stand against a mob / Its people's heart, too small to hold a sob" (2–4). The first two lines seem to suggest that Scottsboro is too blind to see its own shameful acts. The third line implies that mob rule still holds power even within the seemingly objective standards of courtroom law. This line also insists on a further lack of remorse and emotional engagement from all members of the community. Scottsboro, personified as human, lacks an outward expression of the shame it should feel, and this outward reflection springs from the dead, small, unfeeling soul that refuses to weep over the injustice it has committed or ignored. Hughes has effectively diminished the stature of the "little" town of Scottsboro by collapsing the court, mob, and townspeople into a heart "too small to hold a sob."

Another poem, "Justice," was originally published in 1923, but it also appeared as the first of four poems published in Hughes's 1932 booklet *Scottsboro Limited*, which was sold to raise money for the Scottsboro Defense Fund (Axelrod, Roman, and Travisano 699). It was the only entry by Hughes not accompanied by a lithograph. The poem plays on the issues of personifying "Justice" as the woman goddess who holds a scale in her hand as she stands blindfolded. She "Is a thing to which we blacks are wise. / Her bandage hides two festering sores / That once perhaps were eyes" (2–4). The blindfold has been cast aside for the more potent image of a bandage. Justice has not voluntarily closed her eyes; instead, her sight has been taken from her. One can hardly ignore the images of lynching. Moreover, in the lynching of Sam Hose, the victim is described as having his "eyes bulge out his sockets." Eyes themselves are strong reminders of a "black victim" who has been "defined precisely as a kind of extinguished witness. Eyes were dangerous possessions in the Jim Crow South" (Gussow 53). It is clear that justice is controlled and threatened by the same types of violent acts that lynching culture already knows.

When asked by the editors of Contempo if he would send them something about the Scottsboro case, Hughes responded with two essays and a poem. In the essay published there entitled "Southern Gentlemen, White Prostitutes, Mill-Owners, and Negroes," Hughes writes: "But back to the dark millions—black and half-black, brown and yellow, with a gang of white fore-parents—like me. If these twelve million Negro Americans don't raise such a howl that the doors of Kilby prison shake until the 9 youngsters come out (and I don't mean a polite howl, either), then let Dixie justice (blind and syphilitic as it may be) take its course, and let Alabama's southern gentlemen amuse themselves burning 9 young black boys till they're dead in the state's electric chair" (*Good Morning Revolution* 58).

More than simply calling on his complex subject position, Hughes is reminding his white audience that white men have a long history of sexual relationships with African American women. It is, of course, the imagined reversal—a black man with a white woman—that is often used to justify lynching as vengeance for rape.[4] But this rationalization masks the historical realities of white "southern gentlemen" raping their black slaves, servants, or sharecroppers. Equally important is the fact that Hughes regards even Dixie "law" to be no more than legalized lynching involving burning young black boys for the entertainment of "southern gentlemen."

The victims in this case were widely denoted as the "Scottsboro Boys." Rather than being given the status they deserve by being recognized as either "defendants" or "men," they were called "boys," an echo of the racist term of address used by white landowners toward slaves. Scottsboro as a place thus signifies a high degree of fear. It is located in the Jim Crow South, is identified with a state known for lynching, and it is a place where Justice herself has fallen victim to violence and mob rule. We know that lynchings were often advertised and publicized to be performed on specific dates. For the lynching of Luther Holbert of Florida (1893), "trains brought in additional participants and spectators from surrounding cities. After a mock trial, the prolonged execution began" (Litwack 15). For Hughes, the court case against these young men in either Scottsboro or Huntsville would be nothing more than the same type of "mock trial."

Citing the date on which one of the Scottsboro Boys (Clarence Norris) was scheduled to be executed (but fortunately never was), Hughes further blurs the distinction between public trial and lynch mob in his poem "August 19th." The details surrounding the exact date of publication for this poem illuminate Hughes's attempt to exert his influence on Norris's fate. Hughes's poem was published on June 28, 1938, in the *Daily Worker*. It is a direct response to the Alabama Supreme Court's ruling earlier in the month that upheld the penalty of the death sentence for Clarence Norris. As such, Hughes's poem addresses this latest pronouncement in the case as something that turns the law into "a lyncher's rope" (83–84). Soon after, Norris's death sentence was commuted to life imprisonment. The events of 1938 provide the best context for this poem, not the first arrest made in 1931.

The publication of Hughes's poem highlights the fact that many sought to save Norris from his impending fate. In fact, not only did Hughes's poem denounce the decision upholding Norris's execution, but it was also published in time to aid in the effort to save his life. Four weeks after the poem's appearance in July 1938, Alabama governor Bibb Graves commuted Norris's sentence to life imprisonment. Hughes's poem contributed to this turn in Norris's fate. This poem also reminds us that there were many turns in Norris's increasingly long case. Norris was offered parole in January 1944 only to violate it by September of the same year for leaving the state with fellow Scottsboro defendant Andy Wright. Norris spent from October 1944 to September 1946 back in jail. Norris was back in the news as late as 1976, when Governor George Wallace officially pardoned him.

Norris's September 1946 parole coincided with that of another defendant in this case. Ozie Powell's case for parole took place in June of that year. Hughes also wrote about Powell. Published in April 1936, his "Ballad of Ozie Powell" alludes to lynching as Hughes refers to the law as nothing more than a "Klansman with an evil will" (11). However, the poem's meaning is elusive outside of its historical context. Again, the 1932 arrest and trials are not the best context in which to read this poem. Rather, the poem references events that transpired four years later. On January 24, 1936, Powell was being transferred back to his Birmingham, Alabama, jail cell after having appeared in court the day before. During this transfer by car, Powell drew a knife and attacked Deputy Edgar Blalock. Powell was later shot in the head by Sheriff Jay Sandlin. Both men survived. But these events alone do not account for the poem's sympathetic attitude toward Powell.

Hughes sympathizes with the plight of Powell because he reads Powell's rage as a natural result of having repeatedly been denied justice. Powell had already served five years for a crime he did not commit. He was also denied his parole the day before his frustration turned to violent rage. This frustration was compounded by the fact that his case was never fully argued before the U.S. Supreme Court. Earlier, on April 1, 1935, the U.S. Supreme Court sided with the defendants because of the notable absence of blacks as jurors in the original case in Alabama. However, a filing error kept this case from actually being tried in Washington. The high court simply called for a retrial within Alabama jurisdiction. So close to getting a more legitimate trial before the U.S. Supreme Court, Powell's case was instead returned to Alabama.

Hughes alludes to this denial in line 13 of the poem when he reprimands the nine men who serve as federal judges in Washington. Moreover, it was not the first time Powell had endured the strange frustration of having simultaneously won *and* lost. As early as 1932, Powell's case set the standard by which all law is now practiced. After this 1932 case, all defendants earned the right to legitimate legal counsel. If a defendant could not afford counsel, the government was required to provide it. This November 1932 case marked the first time in legal history that such counsel was ruled mandatory.

Hughes's sympathy for Powell grew out of an understanding of Powell's frustration. Powell's act of rage is contextualized against never having committed the crime to begin with, having to worry about possibly being pulled from his cell and lynched, in effect winning his case on two different instances before the U.S. Supreme Court, serving five long years in jail, and now being returned to jail in Alabama.

The retaliation of shooting Powell in the head is what Hughes is referencing in the first and last stanza of the poem when he suggests that Alabama ground is now even more red for having shed Powell's blood. There is further reason why the retaliation against Powell caused this poetic anger: after having already subdued Powell after he attacked a deputy, the car he was traveling in was stopped, and Sheriff Sandlin fired a calculated shot aimed at Powell's head. Powell was not shot during the chaos of his attack on the deputy, but instead he was the deliberate target of Sandlin's attempted roadside execution. Having survived, Powell now faced legitimate assault charges. The horrific irony of the outcome intensified when Powell was convicted of assault on July 24, 1937, and thereby sentenced to twenty years in prison. The very next day, rape charges against four other defendants in the case were finally dropped. Had he not attacked a deputy, Powell likely would have had the rape charges against him dropped, too. Powell would not know freedom again until he received parole in June 1946, after spending a total of fifteen years in prison.

Hughes also published a second essay in *Contempo* during 1931. In this essay, Hughes makes repeated references to the situation at Scottsboro by alluding to the various events surrounding the crucifixion of Christ. Pilate's name is mentioned no fewer than three times. Because the residents in Scottsboro will listen only to mob rule, Hughes mocks his listeners by invoking a call-and-response technique that captures the essence of African American culture and demands justice on the mob's own violent terms: "*Listen, guard: Let them out. / Guard with the keys, let 'em out. / Guard with the law books, let them out*" (*Good Morning Revolution* 59). Continuing the allusion to Pontius Pilate and Christ, Hughes states:

Daily, I watch the guards washing their hands. The world remembers for a long time a certain washing of hands. The world remembers for a long time a certain humble One born in a manger—straw, manure, and the feet of animals—standing before Power washing its hands. No proven crime. Farce of a trial. Lies. Laughter. Mob. (60)

The burden that Hughes has to bear is suggested by the final two words of the essay where he writes:

White guard.
The door that leads to DEATH.
Electric chair.
No song. (60)

Hughes is in the process of discovering just how important a song is. These citizens and this cause are in dire need of a song and a singer. They need a poet. A poem.

The poet will be Hughes, and the poem he writes at this time is

"Christ in Alabama." On the night of November 19, 1931 (the same day that the poem was published in *Contempo* with an accompanying illustration by Zell Ingram), Hughes read his poetry in Gerrard Hall on the campus of the University of North Carolina at Chapel Hill.[5]

Hughes avoided being completely mobbed because the editors of the locally published *Contempo*, Anthony Buttitta and Milton Abernethy, waited to release the five thousand extra copies they had printed of this issue until the day Hughes appeared. However, the day was not without incident, as Hughes inadvertently passed for Mexican at a local restaurant: friends accompanying him recall the server later tried to "catch us in a place or two and sock us in the jaw" when he discovered that Hughes was black (Rampersad 1: 225). Hughes was later told that this marked the first time a black man had ever eaten at a table in the dining room of one of Chapel Hill's restaurants (*CW* 14: 77).

Moreover, tension filled the air in the days before the reading. Numerous letters protesting Hughes's appearance were sent to university president Frank Porter Graham. The Carolina Inn refused to let Hughes and Zell Ingram have a room to sleep in during their stay, and they were forced to spend the night with a local black minister (Buttitta 164). More importantly, Hughes was originally scheduled to read on campus in the larger and more prominent Memorial Hall. When he was refused, a "campus demonstration for freedom of speech" ensued, and Hughes was then allowed to read at the smaller and far less prestigious Gerrard Hall (Buttitta 164).

It was no small task to diffuse the tension in the hall that evening. Beginning at 8:30 P.M., Hughes followed the all-black Silver Tongue Quartet ("Negro Poet" 1). He then delivered "a straightforward, humorous story of his life" ("Negro Lecturer" 1). As Hughes stood in Gerrard Hall, he may have felt the conservative power structure of the university. The building itself was built in 1822, and it stood adjacent to what is still the campus's most visible icon, the Old Well. Dr. Guy B. Johnson of the university's Sociology Department introduced him, and the president of the campus chapter of the YMCA presided over the meeting. Perhaps sensing that this was not the place to initiate even further controversy that could reflect poorly on those who had invited him, Hughes appears to have diffused this tension by using humor. He physically passed through this potential danger by disarming the crowd with his easygoing manner. Moreover, he did not read "Christ in Alabama" that evening.

While it appears the evening went without incident, the aftermath of

Hughes's visit highlights the controversial nature of his poem. Although Hughes was scheduled to visit Johnson's 8:30 A.M. sociology class the day after his reading to discuss the subject of the "Negro," Hughes left town prematurely that same morning without attending. Hughes's departure was unexpected. He was apparently so anxious to leave that he skipped the opportunity to receive payment for his visit. Johnson therefore mailed the funds to Hughes, who personally acknowledged receiving the check in the amount of $32.50. Johnson had raised the funds from twenty-five individual donors who each gave between fifty

Fig. 2.2. Langston Hughes and Anthony Buttitta, Franklin Street, Chapel Hill, North Carolina, 1931, from folder 116, Contempo Records #4408, Southern Historical Collection, Wilson Library, The University of North Carolina at Chapel Hill.

CONTEMPO

A Review of Books and Personalities

Volume 1. Number 13   Dec. 1, 1931, Chapel Hill, N. C.   Ten Cents a Copy

Lynching by Law or by Lustful Mob North and South: Red and Black

By LINCOLN STEFFENS

The first time I heard of the now famous Scottsboro case, the narrator told how those colored boys under sentence saw it. And they saw what they saw of it from a rear car. There was some sort of a row—a scrap—or a fight going on in a car so far ahead that they could get glimpses of it only as the train bent around the curves till, by and by, the train stopped. Then they saw a lot of the fighters jump off that front car and run away. They went up forward to hear more about it.

It was later, when the train arrived at its destination, that those witnesses of the incident, were arrested as the scrappers and—rapists. They were so dazed that they never quite recovered from their frightful astonishment.

But you don't have to go by this casual alibi. Take the record of the trials, the speed of them, the ages of the convicted and the circumstances, and one can realize for himself that there was no justice in these cases. There was the opposite. There was righteousness in it.

In Alabama and some parts of the South the more respectable people are yielding to the Northern clamor against lynching. There is lynching in the North, too, but it is not against blacks. It is against the Reds. And it is not by mobs. It is by the police, the courts and juries; and therefore legal, regular, righteous. The righteous people of the South have been gradually waking up to the idea that they can save their face by taking justice out of the rude hands of the mob and putting it in the delicate hands of the lawyers, and judges and a few representatives of the better people in a jury. That is to say, they can lynch their blacks the way the superior North, West and East get their Reds.

Well, now, you can see that the Alabama righteous must feel the Scottsboro case was a perfect example of the new ideal of justice modelled on the great (anti-) Red North. They had some blacks in a jam where the whites might have wreaked their fear of the colored folk by a deeply satisfying lynching. And they did not

(Continued on page four)

Revolts and Rackets

By LOUIS ADAMIC

In a sense *The Populist Revolt* is a timely book. Its subject is—remotely—of current interest. It deals with the expansion, overproduction, underconsumption, unemployment, misery, falling prices, agricultural and bank failures—the familiar cycle of boom, deflation, depression—which produced or accompanied the so-called Populist Movement of the 'eighties and 'nineties. It tells of its picturesque leaders from the South and West—of "Pitchfork" Ben Tillman of South Carolina, "Sockless" Jerry Simpson and Mary Elizabeth Lease ("the Patrick Henry in petticoats") of Kansas, "Bloody Bridles" Waite of Colorado, Watson of Georgia, Macune of Texas, Weaver of Iowa, Ignatius Donnelly of Minnesota, and others. Their fantastic movement for farm and labor relief left permanent marks on America's business and political organization.

Christ in Alabama

By LANGSTON HUGHES

Christ is a Nigger,
Beaten and black—
O, bare your back.

Mary is His Mother—
Mammy of the South,
Silence your mouth.

God's His Father—
White Master above,
Grant us your love.

Most holy bastard
Of the bleeding mouth:
Nigger Christ
On the cross of the South.

Notes from Nowhere

Langston Hughes, prominent poet and novelist, is soon to be the guest of the editors of CONTEMPO * * * Phillips Russell, of historical and literary biography fame, recently married Cara Mae Green, sister of Paul Green of *The House of Connelly* * * * William Faulkner while guest of CONTEMPO was surprised to learn that the University of North Carolina library cannot afford a copy of any of his novels * * * And while we are local, a John Reed Club has come, and the Carolina Playmakers are sponsoring a Theatre Guild production of *Elizabeth the Queen* * * * When the first version of Archibald Henderson's *Shaw* appeared, Max Beerbohm made cartoons and caricatures out of the illustrations and by changing words cleverly mutilated the text to create idiotic meanings. This copy of the book is now in the hands of the heirs of the late William Archer * * * Presidential prospects for 1932 are having a time at getting their new books blurbed in the various literary journals and reviews; they all seem to have memoirs or exposé items * * * Barrett H. Clark will contribute a regular theatre feature to CONTEMPO * * * And now Cape and Smith part the way, but Hal Smith, maker of Cape and Smith in America, is to make a prominent Harrison Smith with such authors as William Faulkner, J. Middleton Murry, Evelyn Scott, Marcus Hindus

Southern Gentlemen, White Prostitutes, Mill-Owners, and Negroes

By LANGSTON HUGHES

If the 9 Scottsboro boys die, the South ought to be ashamed of itself—but the 12 million Negroes in America ought to be more ashamed than the South. Maybe it's against the law to print the transcripts of trials from a State court. I don't know. If not, every Negro paper in this country ought to immediately publish the official records of the Scottsboro cases so that both whites and blacks might see at a glance to what absurd farces an Alabama court can descend. (Or should I say an American court?) . . . The 9 boys in Kilber Prison are Americans. 12 million Negroes are Americans, too. (And many of them far too light in color to be called Negroes, except by liars.) The judge and the jury at Scottsboro, and the governor of Alabama, are Americans. Therefore, for the sake of American justice, (if there is any) and for the honor of Southern gentlemen, (if there ever were any) let the South rise up in press and pulpit, home and school, Senate Chambers and Rotary Clubs, and petition the freedom of the dumb young blacks—so indiscreet as to travel, unwittingly, on the same freight train with two white prostitutes . . . And, incidently, let the mill-owners of Huntsville begin to pay their women decent wages so they won't need to be prostitutes. And let the sensible citizens of Alabama (if there are any) supply schools for the black populace of their state, (and for the half-black, too—the mulatto children of the Southern gentlemen. [I reckon they're gentlemen.]) so the Negroes won't be so dumb again . . . But back to the dark millions—black and half-black, brown and yellow, with a gang of white fore-parents—like me. If these 12 million Negro Americans don't raise such a howl that the doors of Kilber Prison shake until the 9 youngsters come out, (and I don't mean a polite howl, either) then let Dixie justice (blind and syphilitic as it may be) take its course, and let Alabama's Southern gentlemen amuse themselves burning 9 young black boys till they're dead in the State's electric chair. And let the mill-owners of Huntsville continue to pay women workers too little for them to afford the price of a train ticket to Chattanooga . . . Dear Lord, I never knew until now that white ladies (the same color as Southern gentlemen) travelled in freight trains . . . Did you, world? . . . And who ever heard of raping a prostitute?

Facts About Scottsboro

By CAROL WEISS KING
(Attorney for Defense)

On March 25, 1931, two white girls, seven white boys and fifteen to eighteen colored boys were hoboing through Alabama on a freight train. As a result of that episode eight of the Negroes, all under 20, have been sentenced to death and the ninth Negro, a boy of 14, is awaiting trial—the jury in his case having disagreed as to whether he should be electrocuted or serve a life sentence.

The uninitiated might suppose that the Negroes had been guilty of some offense warranting the severe penalty which the Circuit Court of Jackson

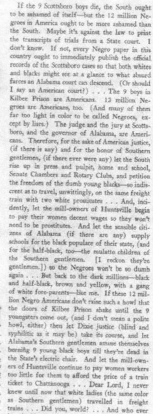

Fig. 2.3. Front page of *Contempo* as it appeared on November 19, 1931. Illustration by Zell Ingram.

cents and $2.50. For Johnson, securing such money was difficult because many people were reluctant to give. They cited two main reasons, stating that "if this is a *Contempo* affair, count me out" and asking, "Are you bringing Mr. Hughes here as a poet or as a communist?"[6]

Even the university was forced to work hard to publicize the fact that it was not directly linked with *Contempo* in any way. In his mistaken belief that the university ran and funded *Contempo*, newspaper publisher Wilton E. Hall of Anderson, South Carolina, went so far as to call on North Carolina governor O. Max Gardner to "take a hand in the management of the magazine" because of Hall's shock in seeing the "red flag of communism defiantly flaunted in the face of Southern Democracy."[7] As many as eleven months after Hughes's visit, reactions to this poem made Hughes the subject of several publications and numerous statewide newspaper editorials. One exchange in the *Charlotte Observer* blatantly stated one man's desire to make an example of Hughes by covering him in a "coat of tar."[8]

Finally, the university's hierarchy collaborated with its official student-led organization to issue a lengthy and formal proclamation asserting the legitimacy of its policies on free speech. Of the five major points outlined in the statement, point number four justified the fact that the publically funded appearance did not trek too far into communist or liberal territory. The statement cited the fact that its guest Langston Hughes did not read "Christ in Alabama" during his official campus visit.

Intentionally distanced from such controversy in the weeks after his visit, Hughes was immediately generous to those who welcomed him to Chapel Hill. Johnson requested permission by mail to distribute copies of "The Negro Speaks of Rivers," complete with a mimeographed image of Hughes's signature to those who had donated the money passed on to the poet. Hughes upgraded the suggested gifts by responding with twenty-five copies bearing his personal signature. The various autographed poems Hughes passed on to Johnson suggest new meanings within the context of Hughes's visit. As requested, Hughes returned copies of "The Negro Speaks of Rivers," a poem with latent overtones to lynching. Furthermore, he also sent "Cross," a poem that highlights the difficulties of being mulatto. As we shall see, perhaps the inclusion of this poem can best be understood as Hughes's means of trying to help readers better understand the issue of miscegenation informing "Christ in Alabama." Hughes also included a handwritten poem he titled "Tomorrow," which appeared under the title "Poem" in *The Weary Blues*. Here Hughes's hope for the future highlights the direction he may hope the university and its youth are taking. In the handwritten version, Hughes included the sometimes missing assertive final line "We march!"[9] Finally, Hughes sent copies of "I, Too." The irony of Hughes *not* being sent to the kitchen to eat while he was at a public restaurant in Chapel Hill was perhaps too much for Hughes to resist.[10]

Hughes himself soon received several concerned letters from those closest to him after other readers saw the poem. Elmer Carter wrote the following in his letter to Hughes: "I have been a little fearful about your safety. The fervor . . . might cause some of the more hot-headed cracker type to attempt to do you bodily harm" (Rampersad 1: 225). On February 10, 1932 (four months after the Chapel Hill appearance), Hughes wrote to Carl Van Vechten: "Friends in the North are writing me that I'll surely be lynched. And my mother has wired that I come back at once: prayers are being said at the altar for me in Cleveland!" (*Remember Me to Harlem* 93).

Hughes's portrayal of a black lynching victim in this poem as Christ crucified captures the historical realities that surrounded earlier lynchings; furthermore, it uses a discourse that looks to the past and contributes to shaping the way future lynchings are described. Ida B. Wells-Barnett describes a moment where a lynch victim was seated upon a throne and treated like a "mock king" (28), and *100 Years of Lynching* contains an excerpt from a lynching in which the victim had a placard hung over his head that read "King of the Jews" (Ginzburg 11). The metaphor is so powerful and seemingly appropriate that even a newspaper editor for the *Kansas City Post-Dispatch* returns to the imagery when he describes the events surrounding the lynching of Cleo Wright on January 25, 1942: "'Another Blot on Missouri' vented the Argus editor, having predicted earlier that 'powerful forces' possessed 'brushes already for a general whitewashing of the case' and officials prepared, like Pontius Pilate, to permit it" (Capeci 56). It is the first and last lines of Hughes's published poem "Scottsboro" that most closely remind us of just how interrelated newspaper headlines, politics, history, culture, and poetry are. The accompanying illustration, which appeared in the booklet *Scottsboro Limited*, shows the eight men's hands and feet bound with ropes and their arms held in a position of crucifixion against the bars of the jail cell. In all capital letters, looking like front-page headlines, Hughes writes in the first line of the poem: "8 BLACK BOYS IN A SOUTHERN JAIL / WORLD, TURN PALE!" (1–2).

By portraying Christ as a black victim of crucifixion, Hughes's poem also engages a long-standing tradition in African American culture of the image of the Black Christ. The roots of the Black Christ can be traced to slavery, where "He was for the slave a fellow sufferer" (Douglas 24). In fact, this image defied the "understanding of Jesus that supported the dehumanization of Black people. The Blackness of this Christ was most evident in the Christ's identification with the black slaves and the condemnation of the White slaveholders" (Douglas 30). As early as 1829, Robert Alexander Young argued that "God will send forth a messiah—born of a black woman—who will liberate Black people" (Douglas 31). Henry McNeal Turner later suggested in 1898 that "We have as much right biblically and other wise to believe that God is a Negro" (176).

By the twentieth century, the Black Christ continued to be invoked in varying ways in the African American tradition. The December 1916 issue of *Crisis* featured a sketch covering pages 78–79 and titled *Christmas in Georgia, A.D., 1916*. The sketch depicts approximately twenty white members of a mob pulling on the ropes of a lynched black man. Hovering behind the lynched figure is a silhouette of Christ. With stones being tossed at the victim, and the biblical inscription, "Inasmuch as ye did it unto the least of these, My brethren, ye did it unto Me" posted on the lynched victim's tree, the victim's association with Christ is clear. The mob ignores its own faults and willingly casts stones as if it were part of a new order of powerful leaders. Later, in 1924, Marcus Garvey introduced his concept of the Black Christ at the convention of the Universal Negro Improvement Association. He asserted that "as a Jew from the line of Jesse, Jesus had 'Negro blood' running through his veins" (Douglas 32).

Among several of his writings, Countee Cullen's poem "Christ Recrucified" (1922) adds to the cultural association between crucifixion, the Black Christ, and lynching: "The South is crucifying Christ again" because "Christ's awful wrong is that he's dark of hue."[11] Cullen continued with such connections through his works *Color* (1925) and *The Black Christ and Other Poems* (1929).

In addition to his understanding of this long tradition of the Black Christ, the conditions surrounding the jail site of the Scottsboro Boys, a place that Hughes had visited in person before writing "Christ in Alabama," are relevant. The scene at the jailhouse where the young men were held is described by newspaper correspondent Nancy Cunard:

[F]or two years, they'd been face to face with the electric chair across the passage in front of their cells and now they had the gallows to stare at in the electric light. On the last step was the trap door to eternity—a painting of Christ at Gethsemane, done by some dead convict, above it. The correspondent looked at the gallows and the Christ. Then he saw the eyes—the Scottsboro boys were looking at him. It was full of noose, shadows of themselves shuffling around, straining ears for the rumble of mobs. They couldn't sleep; they were wondering all [the] time if they would die in Decatur, lynched, or be convicted again. (277)

Cunard's description reminds us that the imagery of Christ's arrest and crucifixion surrounded these young men for more than two years. Moreover, the very real threat of lynching haunted this scene where at least "two lynch mobs had already started out from Huntsville and Scottsboro," intent on lynching either the witnesses, Ruby Bates and Lester Carter, or the defendants themselves (277). Only the "militia posted across the roads outside of Decatur" prevented a literal lynching from occurring (277).

In addition to capturing and further spreading the imagery that links crucifixion with lynching, "Christ in Alabama" also demonstrates Hughes's desire to reach multiple audiences with his song. Readers from various classes and races recognize the explosive overtones of Hughes's metaphor. Hughes's "simultaneously political and poetic effectiveness thus results from his ability to reach multiple audiences in a variety of contexts" (Thurston, "Black Christ" 31). Ironically, this varied audience was later excluded from finding the poem in the 1959 edition of Hughes's *Selected Poems*, one consequence of the 1953 investigations by the House Committee on Un-American Activities (HUAC), which caused Hughes to deliberately avoid publishing such poetic statements.

This poem contains the voices of many speakers. It follows what Mikhail Bakhtin calls *novelization*, as the typically monologic discourse of poetry seeks to incorporate the dialogic force of the novel:

Christ is a nigger,
Beaten and black—
O, bare your back.

Mary is His mother—
Mammy of the South,
Silence your mouth. (1–6)

In the context of lynching, the word "black" does not necessarily denote race. "Black" literally implies the charred remains of a lynch victim. His body is now black, not brown, because it has been burned. Hughes uses "black" in this way in "Question" (1922), when he speaks of a "black torso" (7). Here the black torso may be all that remains after the body has been burned. Remembering Hughes's lament for a song in his *Contempo* essay, the silencing mentioned in the sixth line also seems significant. Connected to the "bleeding mouth" (11) mentioned in the final stanza, the implication is that speaking results in receiving a blow to the mouth. The illustration itself highlights three areas with bright white color against a black silhouette of a man. Two of the highlights fall on the man's palms to indicate scars where nails went through, but one illuminates the man's mouth, which suggests the importance of sound and speech. Such a man must break through a double silence that suppresses him from speaking. These victims are the dead and the living who continue to live with oppression and the constant fear of violence. Hughes's call to be the singer of this song and the poet of lynching poems counters this attempted silencing through the most forceful use of art he knows.

Hughes's reference to "Mary" and the "*Mammy of the South*" is also important. In fact, Taylor's illustration for this poem, which appeared in *Scottsboro Limited*, featured an image of a "Mammy" in the background behind a black figure fronting a cross. The cross and the cotton are white as if to suggest the greed of the white plantation owner. It appears that this "Mammy" and the Virgin Mary "both had husbands that were not the fathers of their child. Christ's father is God, and the father of the mammy's child is the white plantation master. Slave Bibles, which the slaves were forced to learn, also emphasized that the plantation master was deific and held all power over the slaves" (Axelrod, Roman, and Travisano 705).

The final two stanzas of the poem complete the imagery and heritage of this victim:

God's His Father—
White Master Above,
Grant us your love.

Most holy Bastard
Of the bleeding mouth:
Nigger Christ
On the cross of the South. (7–13)

By capitalizing the H in "His," Hughes suggests that this victim is also holy. Multiple voices speak within the poem: "The unassuming typographical device of italic script brings to this deceptively simple poem all the interpretive uncertainty of mob psychology. Lines in both roman and italic type offer "multiple subject positions that, like a Union Square protest rally, are crowded with potential speakers" (Thurston, "Black Christ" 34). The poem, like the essays written for *Contempo*, sheds light on Hughes's vision of just how unjustified many of these lynchings are. The poem spends nearly half of its stanzas creating the impression that this victim, like Christ, is a mulatto of sorts. His mother is black, and his father is white. Hughes's choice to pass on signed copies of his poem "Cross" seems to further highlight this point.

The powerful irony of this poem rests in the fact that Hughes has undermined the essential myth of lynching and the Scottsboro case: neither lynching nor legal lynchings are ever a just response. Although blacks were often accused of raping white women, the poem reminds readers that there are many more white "masters" who have brought children to the world through black women. Hughes effectively undermines the myth that black men rape white women by troping on the image of Christ. In his metaphor, God is likened to a white male plantation owner who lynches others as a result of a personal understanding of the sexual aggression he knows to be present within himself.

After the final lines of the poem, readers of *Contempo* probably would have turned their gaze back to Ingram's illustration one more time. In reflecting on the incompleteness of its details that still suggest a black human form, they might have noted "in its featurelessness, the infinite repeatability of racist violence" (Thurston, "Black Christ" 38). Later responses to the poem defy logic and reason. One of Chapel Hill's leading citizens responded to the poem by saying: "It's bad enough to call Christ a bastard. But when he calls him a nigger, he's gone too far!" (*CW* 14: 76).

The publication of this highly controversial poem forever changed *Contempo*'s relationship with its advertisers and readers. A careful study of what happened to the publication in the wake of publishing this poem provides a measurable way to document what it means to be controversial. The June 1931 issue of *Contempo*, which appeared before the "Christ in Alabama" issue, featured exactly ten advertisements in its pages. Two issues after the magazine's publication of Hughes's controversial poem, the January 1932 issue featured only one ad. Future issues of *Contempo* offered their own pseudo-ads in which they drew attention to their plight by printing that "little can be expected from local advertising" and "Local Advertising Completely cut." Although *Contempo* eventually weathered the loss of their advertising dollars, the situation was not quickly amended, as only three ads total made their way into the July 5, 1932, issue. *Contempo*, like Hughes, paid a dear price for carrying the flag to the field for this particular battle.

To offer Christ crucified as a metaphor for a lynching when none of the defendants were lynched is a creative move on Hughes's part. It is also an important reminder of the cultural context surrounding the case. The two articles that flank Hughes's poem in the pages of *Contempo* make explicit connections between the notion of lynching and this trial. One writer remarks that in this case the South is trying to "lynch their blacks" (Steffens 1), and another notes that "to lynch by law was as bad as to lynch by the obscene hands of a lustful mob" (King 4). Two issues earlier in *Contempo*, Theodore Dressier asked if the mob of ten thousand spectators outside the courthouse made "the trials of the . . . defendants only slightly above a lynching" (1). John Dos Passos also wondered if the citizens of Alabama were merely enjoying the "pleasure of a legal lynching" (1). Finally, a cartoon also made the connection between lynching and the trial. It included a vulture with a gavel in its claws seated atop a lynching pole to suggest that this trial was merely another form of lynching.

In short, this repeated cultural evidence suggests that Hughes clearly did not invent the connection between lynching and this case. Nor was he the first to apply the word "lynching" to a broader idea of racial injustice that did not end in being hung from a noose. He was part of an even larger cultural moment that consistently expanded the definition of lynching. However, the publication of "Christ in Alabama" marks an important poetic moment where this particular social evolution of the term is denoted. Whereas the term once referred to the thirty-nine lashes of the whip struck on the back of a horse thief, it appears to have morphed once again around this time. The ever-expanding concept of lynching was something to which Hughes would return again throughout his lifetime spent writing against lynching.

Moreover, Hughes would again return to linking lynching with crucifixion. Two of these occasions came during dramatic performances in *Esther* and *The Gospel Glow*. Hughes's libretto *Esther* inserts lynching imagery and symbolism into its retelling of the biblical account of Jewish persecution. In this 1956 production, he invokes the plot of the story to

Fig. 2.4. (*above and opposite*) June 1931 issue of *Contempo* featuring ten advertisements.

make two noteworthy allusions to American lynching culture. Because the original story of *Esther* (as well as the version staged here) calls for Haman to order and arrange for Mordecai to suffer his death by hanging from a gallows, Hughes subtly uses this event to allude to a title used among the Ku Klux Klan. Haman, the man who orders Mordecai's hanging, is titled "the Grand Vizier." While Islamic culture denotes such a political title for men such as Haman, the term also appears to verbally pun on the KKK's position of "Grand Wizard."

Such irony would have been felt most by those who recognized Hughes's allusion to Billie Holiday's rendition of "Strange Fruit" in this same play. Though the song was written by Abel Meeropol more than twenty years before, Hughes slyly alludes to this Jewish man's lyrics when he allows Haman the opportunity to sadistically revel in the prospect of seeing Mordecai hang. Hughes has Haman say:

Let his eyes be eyes
For the crows to pluck
And his lips be lips
For the wind to suck. (CW 6: 123)

Hughes's rhyme between "pluck" and "suck" suggests an all-too-similar rhyme in lines 9 through 10 of "Strange Fruit." Hughes did not miss an opportunity to enact poetic justice on this Grand Wizard by making him suffer the very fate he deemed appropriate for another. Perhaps black audience members felt a measure of deeper understanding for Jewish culture and the concept of *contrapasso* as they envisioned the contemporary plight of lynching as a powerful analogue for Queen Esther's heroism.

Hughes invoked a similar strategy again in his 1962 play *The Gospel*

Fig. 2.5. December 15, 1932, issue of *Contempo* featuring one advertisement.

Glow. Premiering approximately seven years after *Esther*, *The Gospel Glow* portrayed what Hughes described as the "first Negro Passion play" (*CW* 6: 354). As such, an elder describes the crucifixion of Christ by saying "they lynched Him on the cross" (*CW* 6: 399). This reference to lynching gives it a resonance among its black church audience members for understanding Christ's martyrdom. Hughes's direct reference to lynching alters how other analogies in the play can be read.

Fig. 2.6. Pseudo-advertisements featured in the December 6 and 15, 1931, issues of *Contempo*.

Audience members also hear an elder recounting what he heard from those who killed Christ: "'Gimme a piece of His garment for a souvenir!' Umm! Casting lots for His garments" (*CW* 6: 399). In addition, the play's repeated references to the forming mob as well as the hanging of the two thieves echo American lynching culture even as they accurately describe biblical events. More telling is the extended description of the resurrection of Lazarus in which the very bones of his dismembered body appear to be reconnected.

These subtle references to lynching are important. According to Leslie Catherine Sanders, "Hughes's gospel plays are his most enduring contribution to American theatre" (353). Considering the worldwide success of Hughes's other plays such as *Mulatto*, this enduring contribution reminds us of Hughes's process in writing these plays. In preparing to write a play such as *The Gospel Glow*, Hughes visited varying churches in Harlem where he witnessed "A mingling of ancient scripture and contemporary problems" (*CW* 6: 353). Like *Esther*, *The Gospel Glow* connects the historic account of Christ's crucifixion with the concept of lynching, thus resulting in Hughes's campaign reaching an international audience.

"The Bitter River"

While Scottsboro is where Hughes's national campaign against lynching culture became so overt that it grew impossible to ignore, it only intensified during the early 1940s. Although it might at first seem surprising, the great majority of Hughes's poems that address lynching were not written in or before the 1930s; rather, they were written between 1941 and 1950. In fact, Hughes addressed lynching during this time period in more poems than he did in the previous two decades combined.

Why did Hughes find it so necessary to address lynching throughout the 1940s? After all, had not the practice of lynching greatly subsided by the 1940s? By one account, the number of lynching victims averaged about three per year in the 1940s (Thompson 123). At least two key cultural factors seem to have contributed to Hughes's poetic outpouring against such injustice: World War II and the failure of antilynching legislation. They are interconnected. The war highlighted U.S. hypocrisy in fighting against racism abroad but not in America, leaving much of the country calling for "double victory" against such practices overseas and at home. Thus, the absence of a true discussion of antilynching legislation was a measurable failure of America to win at home as it had appeared to win in Germany and Japan.

World War II also brought with it a hardening of racism in many communities. Dominic Capeci's study on the lynching of Cleo Wright in Missouri on January 25, 1942, has uncovered a significant psychological connection between the world war and the mentality of lynchers. Speaking specifically in regard to the events surrounding this lynching in Sikeston, Missouri, Capeci notes:

> Lynchers spoke openly of their duty to take the life of a would-be rapist for having attacked the wife of a soldier "off defending the United States." . . . Small wonder lynchers combined individual "psychic compensation" and "community honor." Like nineteenth-century mob members incapable of supporting their families in the midst of economic depression, Sikeston men unable, unwilling, or not yet called to serve abroad discovered their self worth in the protection of womenfolk. Possibly some of them . . . experienced guilt or frustration at neither being in uniform nor protecting the home front adequately. . . . Local and statewide apologists equated Wright's violence with Japan's attack on Pearl Harbor and, by inference lynchers with men in the armed forces. Both crimes made "American blood boil for revenge," and the executioners—troopers in combat—took steps to make it difficult for "negroes, or Japs to molest them or their families" further. (171)

The lynching of fourteen-year-old Cleo Wright occurred during 1942, and it should also be noted that Howard Walsh was murdered in Laurel,

Mississippi, during this same year. Wright's lynching became "a matter of international importance" as the details of the event were broadcast on short wave radio to Germany and Japan before being relayed to the Dutch East Indies and India. Listeners were told: "If the democracies win the War, here is what the colored races may expect of them" (Rotnem 238–39).

In addition, this period marked a dramatic decline in the national efforts to pass antilynching laws as attention shifted away from American brutality and toward Germany's. While the years 1934 to 1940 saw more than 130 such laws brought before the legislative bodies of the United States, the years 1941 to 1951 saw only 66 introduced in Congress (Zangrando 165). In fact, not a single antilynching bill came before Congress in 1941 or 1942 (Zangrando 165), and Hughes's passionate desire to keep the subject of lynching alive in the nation's consciousness during this period is a reminder of his heroic choice to counter such legal failings with poetry. Though antilynching bills passed in the House on three occasions (1922, 1937, and 1940), no bill was ever approved by the full Congress during this time (Zangrando 212).

Why did Hughes continue his campaign against lynching well into the 1940s? Perhaps he felt that three lynching victims per year were still too many. Moreover, "we need only to study the NAACP's photographic archive from the 1940s and 1950s to know that lynching remained a clear and present danger to African Americans" (Goldsby 288). Such images from this archive also remind us that lynching culture had shifted its practices away from murder and toward maiming during this period. In these photographs, we see "lynching's reappearance in blindings, amputations, and other corporal mutilations" (Goldsby 288–89).

"The Bitter River" best represents Hughes's lifelong commitment to singing out against lynching. This poem was published in the same year (1942) that Cleo Wright and Howard Walsh were lynched. As mentioned, Hughes's texts address lynching culture through references to sunlight and rivers. As Michael Bennett has stated so persuasively, African American texts often complicate simple portrayals of natural beauty because "a black literary tradition . . . from its very inception[] has constructed the rural-natural as a realm to be feared for specific reasons and the urban-social as a domain of hope" (198). Just as Bennett discusses what he calls a tradition of the antipastoral found in *Narrative of the life of Frederick Douglass, An American Slave*, Langston Hughes's canonical poem "The Bitter River" can also be contextualized within the framework of an Anglo-European pastoral tradition.

Hughes's choice to invoke the general notion of the pastoral form itself is a powerful assertion that demonstrates his ability to revise Anglo-European models in ways that subvert the dominant culture's position of his time by positing his own ahistorical vision of "American" events.

Written in remembrance of two fourteen-year-old boys, Charlie Lang and Ernest Green, who were lynched at the Shubuta Bridge on Mississippi's Chickasawhay River after being falsely suspected of attempted rape, "The Bitter River" serves as Hughes's longest poetic response to lynching. Unfortunately, it was not the first time a lynching had occurred at this site. In fact, this "was the seventh reported lynching in the Shubuta locality in recent years" (Thompson 122). Locally, this bridge was referred to as the "Hanging Bridge," and its name is highly significant. White children grew up thinking the word "hanging" referred to the fact that it was a suspension bridge, while black children understood the term as a clear reference to the fact that this bridge was a place where people were lynched (Osborn 10–11).

In addition to the seven more recent lynchings, one of the very worst occurred at the "Hanging Bridge" on December 20, 1918. Two men, Andrew Clark (age fifteen) and Major Clark (age twenty) and two pregnant sisters, Maggie Howze (age twenty) and Alma Howze (age sixteen), were lynched from this same bridge after Dr. E. L. Johnston was found murdered. Each of the women was about to bear Dr. Johnston's child. When Major Clark made his intentions of marrying Maggie clear, an argument between Clark and Dr. Johnston ensued. In a very complex turn, Johnston was then murdered by a "white man who had his grudge against Johnston and who felt he could safely kill the dentist and have the blame fall on the Negro [Clark]" (Thompson 70). During the lynching, all four victims denied any wrongdoing. Maggie proved so physically strong that a monkey wrench was used, which left a deep cut on her head and broke her teeth. Despite being struck with the wrench, she climbed back up the bridge at least twice "before someone threw her over the third time" (Mason 105). Furthermore, Alma's unborn baby did not die immediately, and three days later, "one could detect its movement within her womb" (Thompson 70).

Hughes's poem draws attention to the lynching of Lang and Green in the epigraph that also supplies the date of their deaths: October 12, 1942. October 12 is Columbus Day, and Hughes aims his alternative story of U.S. violence at the current national constructions of origins and history. With significant Christian overtones, which include the symbolic importance of crucifixion, the reference to Columbus Day becomes an important entry point for reading the poem. It reminds readers how the discovery of America adversely affects African Americans.

"The Bitter River" extends the concept of crucifixion because these "lynched boys / From its iron bridge hung" (11–12) are sacrificial figures themselves. It is ironic that this bridge has been listed on the National Register of Historic Sites as a result of its significant architectural and engineering design, rather than for the act that Hughes brings to our attention.[12] U.S. lynching culture often hung victims from bridges for several reasons. Although lynchings during this time were not considered criminal cases in courts of law, these neutral territories could never be linked to any one citizen, which assured that no one family could be held accountable for the incident.

Furthermore, such sites served as important monumental space for the community. These easy-to-find landmarks reinforced white superiority as design, construction, and control of these areas was reaffirmed by the act of lynching. Much like a parade, the dead body hung like a banner announcing to all the world in lynching code that "white women are protected here" (Osborn 9). Finally, bridges served as very practical places for a lynching. Sometimes the victim was captured in the nearby river during his attempt to elude the keen sense of smell possessed by the lynch mob's dogs. Also, if the rope should break, the victim could be drowned in the river below.

Elements of topophilia and topophobia comingle at this site. The events demonstrate how these emotions need to be sifted: "The boys were in the habit of playing with the [white] girl at various times and they played under the bridge. This day they were running and jumping when the girl ran out from under the bridge and the boys behind her. A passing motorist saw them" (Thompson 122). It appears that the three children felt a rush of joy from the physical activity of "running and jumping." It is not hard to imagine that each also felt a certain thrill from the dangers associated with exercising in the fearful shadow of this well-known bridge. But the water, sunshine, and activity that brought them a feeling of place affection also activated a fear in the "passing motorist." The driver may have feared, at worst, that the boys intend to sexually attack the young girl; at best, these boys were overstepping racial boundaries.

This complex juxtaposition of emotions does not end there. The boys were held at the Quitman jail on charges of "attempted assault of a white girl" (Thompson 122). Once removed from the jail, the boys were lynched from the Shubuta Bridge, where their "reproductive organs were cut off" (Thompson 122). Notice how the emotional resonance of this place shifts during the mob's lynching: the victims' once playful fear has now become overwhelmingly real, and the mob's fear that such young men are sexual predators is abated through castration and execution. But even this sense of satisfaction must be tempered by the reality that such lynchings offer only a temporary reprieve from such fears. After all, the mob had been here several times before and no doubt must have realized that they would be forced to return again. Such an emotional shift is complete only when the young girl herself realizes her attitude toward this riverplace is now a place of growing fear where games can be misinterpreted. Finally, many passersby and local residents will balance such emotions in varying degrees. Potential victims may fear this monumental space's ability to intimidate while simultaneously feeling relief that their lives have not been taken from them. White community members may recall the importance of seizing upon such lynching opportunities to again shift their fears toward young black men.

In returning to "The Bitter River," we note the ambiguity of the phrase the bridge "*crosses* the stream" (59, emphasis added). The speaker of the poem is figuratively crucified by having to experience the sheer horror of the scene. The poem conveys such connotations in surprising proportions as we are told: "I've drunk of the bitter river / And its gall coats the red of my tongue" (9–10). The image of "gall" is again activated in line 57, in which the speaker has had to "drink of the bitter cup / Mixed with blood and gall" (56–57).

The final reference to "gall" emphasizes the speaker's suffering and the fact that he feels a strong desire to remember the events of this present time at this particular place. "Gall" certainly appears to be an allusion to Christ's suffering on the way to his own crucifixion. Matthew 27:34 records that "There they offered Jesus wine to drink, mixed with gall; but after tasting it, he refused to drink it." Extending this connection further, we find that the blood of these two boys also evokes the wine mentioned in Matthew when Hughes writes that the gall has "mixed with the blood of the lynched boys" (11).

While the actual reason for Christ's refusal to drink the gall may be uncertain, the traditional understanding of this act becomes central to

Hughes's poem: "Tradition says that the women of Jerusalem customarily furnished the painkilling narcotic to prisoners who were crucified. Jesus refused to drink it because he wanted to be fully conscious until his death" (Barker 1487). Here, Hughes's speaker is conscious of the violence and the place in which it occurs. Indeed, Hughes himself had begun to taste the figurative blood of these boys: during this time he was being pursued by the FBI for his suspected communist associations.

This reading supplies us with a contextual understanding of why Hughes spends so much time in the poem enumerating a long litany of prisoners. While staring into this river, Hughes seems to be reminded of his visit to Kilby prison nearly eleven years earlier when he mentions seeing the "dark bitter faces behind steel bars" (27). In his first autobiography, Hughes describes his disappointing personal interaction with the Scottsboro Boys in 1931:

> Over Alabama that winter lay the shadow of Scottsboro. But I heard no discussion whatsoever of the case at Tuskegee, although at nearby Kilby eight of the nine Negro boys involved were in the death house where I went to see them. (The ninth boy, only thirteen years old, had had a mistrial and was in prison in Birmingham.) Their chaplain, a small-town Negro minister, said it might cheer the boys up if I would read them some of my poems. So at Kilby prison I went down the long corridor to the death house to read poetry to the Scottsboro boys. In their grilled cells in that square room with a steel door to the electric chair at one end, in their gray prison uniforms, the eight black boys sat listlessly in their bunks and paid little attention to me or the minister as we stood in the corridor, separated from them by bars. Most of them did not even greet us. Only one boy came up to the bars and shook hands with me. (*CW* 14: 90)

In this visit, the young men seem to have nearly given up all hope of being exonerated. Furthermore, it is important to note how energized Hughes was by this case, as their figurative lynching is still on his mind eleven years after they were first arrested.

In addition to the Scottsboro Boys, Hughes mentions other important prisoners in "The Bitter River." The African American educator Lewis Jones was arrested while "working on recording African American songs in Mississippi for a WPA project for the Library of Congress." Hughes again reminds us that Alabama had become a violent place when he cites the "voteless share-cropper" (30). Many sharecroppers had been killed, jailed, or injured there in 1931 when "the local police raided a secret meeting of the Alabama Share Cropper's Union on July 15." This meeting was organized in an effort to demand the release of the Scotts-boro Boys and "several [members] were lynched afterwards" (Axelrod, Roman, and Travisano 705). The poem's reference to "a soldier thrown from a Jim Crow bus" (32) is best contextualized against Capeci's comments about the events surrounding Cleo Wright's murder in Sikeston. It serves as a reminder of the added psychological tension surrounding lynching during World War II.

Hughes also states that this "bitter river reflects no stars" (37). Based upon Hughes's use of star imagery throughout his poetry, a river that "reflects no stars" is a river that offers no consolation of freedom in being crossed. Moreover, the syntactic repetition of the phrase "behind steel bars" (27–33) not only draws the reader's attention toward the extended list of prisoners (seeing wrongful imprisonment as a larger extension of lynching), it also suggests the varying ways in which African Americans were lynched/crucified in American society. Hughes is suggesting that the penal system functions as a system of cages holding the next bodies to be disposed. It treats African Americans like waste.

In addition, the call-and-response nature of the repetition of "behind steel bars" in the terminal position of these lines suggests that Hughes is asking his listener to engage in a form of communal remembrance that simply must be painful, not tempered with wine and gall. In short, the reader is given a glimpse into the various reasons a drink from "the bitter cup" has been so necessary. The fact that the speaker regrets his past acceptance of the cup mirrors the reality that many readers are less than fully conscious of lynching and must undergo pain when remembering these lynched boys and the thousands they represent.

Hughes's environmentally informed insistence that the river is filthy and muddy displays a unique awareness. He states no fewer than three times that this river "reflects no stars," implying the environmentally unsound practice of dumping human bodies as well as other waste materials in this river. While the image of the "star" appears consistently in his poetry and is linked with notions of freedom, a recognition of the fact that African Americans are being hung like fruit from trees, deposited like waste materials in rivers, and burned like animals during the inhuman act of lynching informs his choice to signify on and reclaim a pastoral tradition that exalts features of the natural world while ignoring how African Americans have been "placed" in such settings.

Read against the context of frustrated efforts to pass antilynch laws, the imagined voices in "The Bitter River" who address the speaker of the poem take on added significance. Hughes writes of being told to "Wait, be patient . . . / Your folks will have a better day" and that "patience / will bring a better day" (38–43). African Americans have been waiting with patience for an antilynching bill since at least 1882, when the first bill was presented to Congress, and no fewer than sixty other bills were proposed by 1931, none of which passed (Zangrando 165). Lynching was, in fact, such a concern in 1896 that President William McKinley supported an antilynching bill in his home state of Ohio and stated that "lynchings must not be tolerated in a great and civilized country like the United States" (Zangrando 15).

A brief overview of antilynching legislation reveals just how such measures had met repeated failure. On January 29, 1901, North Carolina congressman George Henry White, an African American, spoke on his earlier attempt to bring forth an antilynching bill that at present "still sweetly sleeps in the room of the committee to which it was referred" (10). White's legislation was followed by future failures to pass such measures. Founded by black women, the self-proclaimed "Anti-Lynching Crusaders" could not help pass the bill of Missouri's Leonidas Dyer, which was initiated in 1918 and filibustered for a week before being dropped in December 1922. What future attempts such as the Wagner-Costigan Bill in 1935 and others afterward proved was that congressional power would prevent the implementation of these measures. Bills were repeatedly stalled by filibusters even as late as 1947.

Counseling the speaker to be patient also suggests the experience of the NAACP's Walter White, who lobbied extensively throughout his life for antilynching bills. In 1933, he had written to Eleanor Roosevelt, enclosing "statements from twenty senators and thirty-two representatives" as well as a report that indicated that fifty-two members of the Senate would vote to pass the Costigan-Wagner Bill against lynching if it could only be brought to the floor for a vote (Zangrando 113). And while Mrs. Roosevelt did set up a meeting for White with her husband, the vote was never called, and the bill could not be passed (114). Three years later, the First Lady continued her communication with White via personal correspondence, encouraging him to contact the "more prominent members of the senate" given the difficulties already encountered in deciding if state or federal policies had constitutional authority in this matter. Despite Mrs. Roosevelt's best intentions, White was essentially told that the overall sentiment of her husband's administration was that it was best to wait until "education," "good citizens," and "public opinion" resolved the matter. Although she could not be of immediate help, she confided in a personal letter to Steven Early, "if I were colored, I think I should have about the same obsession he [Walter White] has."

Again, national polls from 1937 found that often more than 70 percent of citizens favored a law that would make lynching a federal crime, yet no laws were ever brought to a vote before the Senate (Zangrando 148). Patience fails the speaker in the poem to the same degree that the U.S. government has failed to enact legislation against lynching American citizens.

Hughes's repeated use of the word "bitter" in "The Bitter River" serves as a reminder of just how powerful this word is in his work. Moreover, it is an important word in Holiday's antilynching song "Strange Fruit," which ends with the line "Here is a strange and bitter crop." In an earlier poem entitled "A New Song" (1933), Hughes uses the phrase "Bitter was the day" (7) three different times. More significantly, one of Hughes's final published poems of 1967 ("Bitter Brew") reveals just how central "The Bitter River" is to his overall oeuvre. In "The Bitter River," Hughes writes:

Yours has been the power
To force my back to the wall
And make me drink of the bitter cup
Mixed with blood and gall. (54–57)

The poet calls up this imagery as he cites one of his last wishes in "Bitter Brew." In "The Bitter River," the speaker is forced to endure the bitter brew and the drink from the cup. "Bitter Brew," published in 1967—the year of Hughes's death and one year before the last recorded U.S. lynching—seeks to reverse the positions of who is forced to drink and prepare the cup. Hughes envisions his own essence reduced to a liquid and placed into a cup after his death. When it is sipped, it will "give the white bellies / The third degree" (16–17).

It is important to remember the full breadth of the songs Hughes has sung. Continuing in the role of self-appointed singer, Hughes reminds his listeners in "The Bitter River" that the speaker has been a "singer of weary song" (71). Rather than singing only jazz and blues lyrics, Hughes has been and will continue to write other powerful tunes. As "Sliver" (1951) reminds us, poetry "Can cut a man's / Throat sometimes" (7–8).

"The Bitter River," like "Sliver," is intent on doing more than serving as compensation for the pains of the day. It is bent on striking back against the powers that have undercut the hope that "work, education," and "patience" could bring. Hughes is much more than a weary bluesman who glorifies the best of Harlem. He is also an agitated disrupter, seeking to expose the violence and injustice performed by white America as he speaks truth to power.

After addressing the fact that there are those who would have the speaker "forget" such atrocities throughout lines 38 to 57 of "The Bitter River," Hughes increasingly turns his attention to the subject of right memory. And while the speaker's noble effort to remember and be conscious yields one of Hughes's longest lyrics, the speaker demonstrates the harmful effects that sleeping, resting, and forgetting may have: "Tired now of the bitter river / Tired now of the pat on the back / Tired now of the steel bars" (74–76). In noting the speaker's obvious physical and emotional fatigue, one can hardly resist seeing the speaker's will to overcome here as a figurative representation of his own crucifying experience. The emphasis on memory can be read against Hughes's own important reminders in one of his later poems, "Shame on You" (1951), where the speaker laments the fact that Harlem has a movie house named after Lincoln, but none after John Brown: "Black people don't remember / any better than white" (8–9). The speaker in "The Bitter River," however, remembers for all of us. Reliving this lynching becomes a cross that the tired speaker bears for his forgetful readers.

Thus the speaker almost becomes the third crucified member of the moment as this small piece of Mississippi is suddenly transformed into an American Golgotha. The speaker, unlike many of our classroom textbooks, refuses to ignore the painful history of lynching. In *Lies My Teacher Told me: Everything Your American History Textbook Got Wrong*, James Loewen notes that lynchings took place as far north as "Duluth, Minnesota" (159). And after sampling twelve different history textbooks in his 1995 study, Loewen finds that not one single photograph of a lynching appeared in any of the books (160). This fact is particularly disturbing in light of the large number of victims who were photographed, and whose pictures were often turned into postcards and sold throughout various periods of the twentieth-century. Moreover, this historical silencing, where so few members of American society know about the particulars of such racial violence, mirrors what historian David Lewis has found as a connection to "the familiar pliant of a generation of German's knowing nothing of the Holocaust" ("Wounds Not Scars" 1253).

Eventually the speaker's fatigue slowly gestures toward a more defiant position. By the end of the poem, the speaker has had enough and, energized by the emotional memories now attached to this place, gathers together enough anger and frustration to overcome the temptations of forgetfulness. There are simply too many lessons, too many lives, too much violence to be ignored, and the past events related to this place must be revisited, must be preserved (at this place), must be overcome (in consciousness). Hughes ends by writing: "I'm tired of the bitter river! / Tired of the bars!" (88–89). The last reference to "bars" points our attention back to the multiple ways to be lynched and the myriad of crucifixions to endure for blacks in this lynching culture. The last lines remind us that imprisonment, lynching, and skewed court rulings are but a few of the intolerable ways African Americans suffer in the United States. The word "bars" itself suggests no fewer than three locations. We are reminded of the steel bars of jail cells, the bars of the bridge from which the two boys' bodies were hanged and to which their lynch ropes were fastened, and the sand bars which often form in the center or edges of a river itself. It seems little coincidence that all three are sites where various forms of lynching occurred.

In the end, the effects of the gall are either wearing off or being overcome as the speaker demonstrates his heroic strength of will. Perhaps the longest and most enduring element of "The Bitter River" rests in its ability to offer a model for its readers. Having admitted to knowing the taste of "blood and gall" throughout the poem, the speaker admittedly serves as an example of the dangers of accepting such a narcotic. We must not dull the pain of remembering that, between 1882 and 1968, at least "4,742 blacks met their deaths at the hands of lynch mobs" and "as many if not more blacks were victims of legal lynchings (speedy trials and executions)" (Litwack 12).

Like legal cases, committees can also masquerade under a cloak of legitimacy that too closely resembles a lynch mob or a corrupt courtroom jury. Hughes learned that mobs now used different contexts for violence: in courtrooms, they were now jurors, and on committees they were House members and senators. Hughes was eventually called to testify before HUAC to pay the price for writing poetry that reflected poorly on America. This lynching took place in Washington, D.C., near the banks of the Potomac River in 1953.

But, talk about it—
You may be
Crucified.

Langston Hughes, "Not for Publication"

3

Negotiating Censorship in the 1950s

Lynching as Analogy

A black-and-white photograph taken during his testimony before the House Committee on Un-American Activities (HUAC) in March 1953 portrays a look of concern on Hughes's face. Hughes even looks somewhat suspicious with his small, thin mustache. His black-rimmed glasses are removed, and his concentration reveals the tension of the moment. As his glasses dangle in the fingers of his left hand, a pack of untouched cigarettes and a clean glass ashtray are placed before him. Hughes's left elbow rests on two books. Each was most likely written by him. In the most prominent section of the photograph, there are three other books stacked flat in the foreground. The top book contains just enough detail to reveal, at the bottom of its cover, the words "by Langston Hughes." The top book has two three-letter words and then another six-letter word that begins with the letter *T*. The book on top of the stack is certainly Hughes's book of poetry published in 1949 titled *One-Way Ticket*.

Fig. 3.1. Hughes testifying before HUAC, March 26, 1953. By permission of AP/Wide World Photos.

It is highly likely that one of the smaller and less visible books directly under his elbow is *Montage of a Dream Deferred* (1951).

During his lengthy testimony, Hughes was not asked about any of the poems that appeared in these two collections. In fact, the committee chose to ignore Hughes's most anti-American poems: there was no discussion about his poems that interrogate American lynching culture. When asked about the ideas expressed in "Goodbye Christ," Hughes may have been attempting to gesture toward his discussion of lynching found in "Christ in Alabama" when he said: "I have written many religious poems, many poems about Christ" (United States 982). More likely, Hughes's reference to Christ referred to a poem of his that appeared in *Crisis* only weeks earlier entitled "Not for Publication." However, bringing up this poem or the potent subject of lynching under such intense circumstances would have been ill-advised. What he really wanted to say might have been similar to his June 21, 1947, article in the *Chicago Defender*, in which the character Simple reveals why he is willing to discuss racism in America before HUAC. Or perhaps he wanted to show anger toward this committee, similar to the anger he expressed in his May 31, 1947, article in which he decried the fact that more than two dozen self-confessed lynchers went unpunished for the death of Willie Earle in Greensville, South Carolina.

Censorship before 1953

Although this 1953 appearance before HUAC was a very public moment of interrogation for Hughes, it was far from the first time he had faced the force of dominant culture. As early as 1940, several of his works had been censored. The specifics of this banishment included three radio plays he attempted to get CBS to broadcast. *The Organizer* and its theme of forming a sharecroppers' union were too controversial in 1940; comparing Americans who used lynch ropes to what one character called "little Hitlers" kept *Brothers* off the air in 1941; and *Pvt. Jim Crow* never made it to production.

Hughes's audience changed because of World War II. As mentioned earlier, his brief radio play *Brothers* (1941) never aired. Part of the reason *Brothers* never aired was because Hughes linked German racism with what was happening in America. Speaking of the parallels between racism in Germany and the United States, Vincent reminds his mother that "We got a few Hitlers at home to lick, too" who have "lynch ropes" (*CW* 6: 487). In the play, Charlie offers the following logic as to why he is invested in the war: "Sure, we got some *little* Hitlers here. But there's no use letting big Hitler get across that ocean to help 'em. For every fifth-columnist we've got with a lynch rope and a Jim Crow car to back him up, Hitler's got a thousand with tanks and dive bombers trying to get over here to help make things worse" (*CW* 6: 489). CBS opposed airing a play whose rhetorical push for engaging in World War II included the notion that it would keep racism from increasing at home. Rather than portraying Hitler as a terror of epic proportions, Hughes cast him as a barometer for measuring the practices of American lynching culture.

The gradual decline in Hughes's lynching poems over this time is also very revealing of the increasing pressure of censorship. As we have already seen, Hughes made numerous overt references to lynching in his poetry before 1951. There are many others as well. With "Open Letter to the South" (1932), Hughes appealed to the poor whites to take owner-ship of the land. One element of this reclamation project included plac-ing the word "FREE" at the base of "every lynching tree" (44). Hughes also linked American lynching culture with the German takeover of Czechoslovakia in 1938. When his poem "Song for Ourselves" was pub-lished in the *New York Post* on September 19, 1938, Germany's Konrad Henelin and Adolf Hitler had laid the groundwork for occupation of a large section of Czechoslovakia, which culminated with the signing of the Munich Agreement later in the same month. In his poem, Hughes referred to the takeover as a lynching.

Hughes's idea of writing "songs" as compensation for the lynched had been used before throughout his collection *A New Song* (1938). In the title poem, Hughes linked poetry and song as reminders of a past that is about to end. One memory from this bitter past is that of being burned and hung from a noose. In this same collection, the final stanza of "Kids Who Die" expresses hope that songs such as this poem will lead to respect and recognition for all who are drowned, dumped, or lynched in swamps and rivers. Hughes hopes that such deaths will ultimately inspire unity among the living.

As we have already seen in the 1940s, Hughes continued to link the events of World War II with the brutality of lynchings in America. "Southern Mammy Sings" (1941) links the international penchant for warfare with the heartless brutality of lynching. The desire for a dou-ble victory appears in many of Hughes's poems from this era as well. Sarcastically, "Song of Adoration" (1943) takes the traditional five-line stanza often associated with the "mad-song" tradition to explore the fact that those who lynch a black man have no fear of ever being sent to prison for the crime. With "Will V-Day Be Me-Day Too?" (1944), Hughes's speaker is a soldier he names G.I. Joe, who openly wonders at one point if he will still be subject to being lynched after the war. In another of his subtle attacks on American lynching culture, Hughes recounts the *Chicago Defender*'s reporting of lynching in "Madam and the Newsboy" (1944). Lynching is presented in the poem as such a com-monplace occurrence that it warrants no more surprise for a reader of the paper than hearing about the marriage between Marva Trotman and Joe Louis.

However, by 1947, Hughes was forced to explore new strategies for responding to lynching in his poetry. His collection *Fields of Wonder*

(1947) does not offer a single overt reference to lynching. This absence is itself very telling. It is as if the end of the war and the government's increased intensity in tracking Hughes's communist affiliations closed the door on such opportunities. As such, this absence suggests the climate of censorship in which Hughes wrote. Perhaps "Poppy Flower" marks the closest Hughes comes to addressing the subject of lynching in this collection. Is Hughes thinking about the different reactions white and black people might have when looking upon a lynch victim as he dies? If so, the poem gives no overt evidence of this.

In sharp contrast to earlier decades, the 1950s saw Hughes pen only four poems that address the subject of lynching. This is by far the lowest number of such poems for any ten-year period in Hughes's creative life. During this time, Hughes was forced to function "within the bitter limits of censorship" (Sanders 475). Furthermore, Hughes fell under FBI surveillance in 1944 and was denounced as a communist by the Senate in 1948. Not even Hughes's editors were immune to such issues of control and power; many of them at Henry Holt were fired for their roles in publishing Hughes's works in 1951 and 1952 as a result of pressure from Texas conservatives (Rampersad 1: 85).

In addition to repeatedly offering public denials that he had ever been a communist, Hughes also asserted that censorship in America took on a racial dimension. Speaking on the subject in May 1957 as an invited guest before the Authors' League of America, Hughes suggested that censorship "begins at the color line" (Rampersad 2: 270). He informed listeners that "Many black writers live abroad . . . [b]ecause the body of little Emmett Till drowned in a Mississippi River and no one brought to justice, haunts them, too" (Rampersad 2: 270).

►•◄

Rather than leave the country or abandon the subject of lynching, Hughes found a means to restrategize his campaign against it. As Donna Akiba Sullivan Harper has asserted, "devoted Hughes scholars know that Hughes's work possesses the illusion of simplicity—a sleight of hand that hides the depth of complex uses of language, psychology, sociology, and history" (1). I also follow Jonathan Scott, who asserts that Hughes did not "escape from politics" during this time, but rather found a "reentry into the political through a different opening" (162). Because of this complex political atmosphere, Hughes's work became "more advanced aesthetically" (Scott 108). Within the suppressive political climate of this era, "Hughes did not lose his subversive nature" (Tidwell and Ragar 9). More specifically, he explored new ways to critique American lynching culture.

Hughes used lynching as an analogy to negotiate the complexities of this political climate. This chapter explores Hughes's use of lynching as an analogy in two of his poems written during this important period from 1951 to 1953. "Not for Publication" (1953) was too volatile to pass into the mainstream press, so Hughes placed it quietly in the black press as well as in two international publications. Recognizing Hughes's use of lynching as an analogy during this era leads to a reconsideration of Hughes's imagery in "Dream Deferred" (1951). Censorship and Hughes's growing appreciation for photography emerged as key touchstones for understanding Hughes's poetry in the early 1950s.

Analogy

I am using the term "analogy" to express the means by which Hughes translated elements from the visual world of photography into the verbal realm of poetry. While the common use of analogy often suggests a similarity between any two seemingly different things, I choose the word "analogy" (rather than "metaphor" or "simile") with the specific intention of activating Sara Blair's use of this lens to open up new readings of African American works composed in the postwar era. Eschewing the tendency to regard still photographs as objective registers for seeing the world, Blair instead invokes Lisette Model's notion of analogy: "in spite of the fact that [the] image represents streets, houses, people," it is "merely an *analogy* of the physical world around us" (Blair 16). Reading photographs as a medium that communicates an analogy differs in key ways from the practice of seeing them as simply documentary images. The concept of documentation creates the illusion that the image can frame its subject from a wholly objective point of view. Such objectivity negates the real presence of the photographer, who, among other things, selects, crops, lights, or even stages the subject matter. Images inherently allow for a variety of ambiguous readings from visually literate readers who have grown savvy and accustomed to interpreting arrested images. In addition to the medium of photography, the rising field of advertising helps to create a familiarity in the relationship between the writer and the highly visual audience of consumer-readers. Art capitalizes on this emerging literacy as refined viewers are made to feel as if they are seeing something anew for the first time, which captures not life as it is but a place as it appears to be.

Photographic analogies work in rather unique ways. My use of the concept of analogy captures the fact that the photographic image does not seek to portray an objective reality so much as it intends to serve as an apt emotional metaphor for its subject matter. Such analogies do not seek to document the real so much as they long to communicate a subject's emotional appeal.

While there are certainly differences, verbal analogies function in surprisingly similar ways to their visual counterparts. Visual and verbal analogies offer their readers a self-reflexive image. By creating such analogies with words that create rather than capture imagery for the reader, African American writers in the postwar era used the increasing influence of photography to create what Blair calls "photo-texts." These photo-texts exchange the register of the photographic into words. At key times, Hughes's poems make use of verbal analogies that have their roots in the visual realm of photography.

"Analogy" becomes a useful term for discussing Hughes's poetry because it accounts for the unmistakable relationship Hughes had with photography during this era. In this chapter, we will see Hughes's use of analogy as he compares lynching with crucifixion, censorship, and unfulfilled dreams. Hughes's ability to use lynching as an analogy also captures the ever-widening reach of lynching culture and reminds us that such imagery is not to be dismissed in Hughes's works as hyperbole. Just as visual photography does not seek to document reality, Hughes's verbal analogies seek to intensify events. His analogies remind us that the influence of lynching in America extends to cultural contexts beyond literal burnings and hangings or hasty courtroom verdicts. Coming from Hughes, a man who knew lynching intimately, such figurative references to lynching supply time-specific cultural commentary. For Hughes's later poems written in response to American lynching culture, these analogies are inherently unstable. Their ambiguity allows the ideas being compared to veil as much as they reveal. They show rather than say; suggest rather than assert. They imply what would be dangerous to state.

Lynching in the Early 1950s

Lynching began to change in the early 1950s. This change had a direct impact on Hughes's references to lynching in his poetry. As a result, this period in America demanded a new perspective on racism. For a brief time in the early years of the decade, documented reports of lynchings waned so much as to appear to be ending. Official records from Tuskegee Institute reported one lynching in 1951 and zero in the years 1952, 1953, and 1954 combined. In fact, 1952 represented the first year since 1892 that no lynchings had been documented and officially recorded in the United States. However, such numbers were also misleading: "Tuskegee Institute recorded 1953 as another lynch-free year today, but said mob violence is no longer a 'valid index' of race relations, and a new formula will be used in the future" ("Tuskegee Report" 5). To many citizens, lynching may have appeared to be disappearing. In actuality, it was merely undergoing yet another significant revision.

Hughes's lack of antilynching poems during this decade does not seem to reflect a disinterested attitude or an acceptance that lynching was no longer an issue. Rather, Hughes's poetry of this period reflects the constraints of censorship he faced in continuing to test how and where to address this uniquely American problem. Despite the absence of large numbers of visible lynch victims, the habits of American lynching culture had been too deeply engrained to simply disappear. Invoking lynching as an analogy became one way to amplify the reemergence of these racist energies as they appeared in new forms.

The long-standing history of lynching allowed Hughes to use the concept of lynching as an idea that warranted substantial cultural power. The modern historian or scholar may be led to worry that the overuse of the concept of lynching to denote too many things actually weakens the term by asking it to carry more meaning than it is capable of bearing. However, the discussion here is intended to revisit the way the term was actually being used in the early 1950s. What we find is a culture beginning to use lynching as a means to adequately communicate the sustained intensity of racism, which continued despite the gradual reduction in victims being hung from tree limbs. Maintaining careful categories of what counted as an official lynching was irrelevant to Hughes and many other African American citizens. What was absolutely necessary was highlighting the fact that a culture steeped in the practice of lynching was capable of implementing other equally intimidating forms of control and oppression. As the black community understood all too well, lynching by rope had briefly come to a statistical end; but dominant culture had enacted a newly emerging form of domestic terrorism against its own citizens as the years 1949–52 saw no fewer than "68 instances of bombing or attempted bombing" in the United States ("Lynching Report" 103). One way to measure the physical, psychological, and emotional toll of such terrorism was to see it and other behaviors as the next wave of control activated by an American culture that had grown to condone and accept the lynching of its black citizens.

"Not for Publication"

Hughes had kept the topic of racial violence alive in his poetry during the 1940s when antilynching legislation attempts waned. Now, as the 1950s marked a brief change in the practices of American lynching culture, Hughes faced even greater challenges in trying to engage this subject. Lynching had waned statistically, and anyone who addressed the topic was subject to attacks of anti-Americanism during an era of red-baiting. No poem captures the interconnectedness of these pressures better than "Not for Publication." Revisiting this poem reminds us that there were messages only certain audiences were willing to receive. "Christ in Alabama" was controversial when published in the 1930s; had it appeared in 1951, it would have received the designation "subversive."

Ironically, Hughes did publish "Not for Publication." It first appeared in the March 1953 *Crisis*. This and each subsequent publication of the poem reminds us of the limits placed on Hughes's verse. Among other things, the poem addresses the subject of censorship. A closer examination of this first appearance in print reveals that Hughes's poem essentially slips into the NAACP's publication *Crisis* with surprising stealth. In fact, neither Hughes's name nor the title of the poem is listed anywhere on the cover or in the table of contents. Two poems by Hughes nonchalantly appear in the leftover space of a section titled "Good News." To the left of the poem is a list of announcements including one that notifies readers that Ralph Ellison has won a National Book Award for *Invisible Man*. Hughes's poem "Africa" appeared next to "Not for Publication." The two poems took up less than a half page in *Crisis*. Placed side by side, racism as depicted in "Not for Publication" makes America shrink in stature in comparison to the emergence of Africa, which is awakening like a god.

In "Not for Publication," Hughes imagines that Christ would be barred from the doors of many churches in America if he were to return as a black man. In many ways, this poem overlaps the use of Christ as a lynch victim first invoked by Hughes in "Christ in Alabama." (In fact, Hughes later linked the two poems by placing them back to back in his final collection, *The Panther and the Lash*, a choice in sequencing that I address more specifically in the conclusion.) Hughes once used this trope to represent the trial of the Scottsboro Boys as a legal lynching; here he again expands on this connection. After asserting that too many churches celebrate their ability to protect racial divisions rather than strengthen their faith, Hughes ends his brief fourteen-line poem ambiguously. In fact, the final three lines of the poem can be read in at least two different ways. One reading would suggest that while a returning black Christ would only be barred from praying in American churches, current black citizens experience much worse circumstances as they are being lynched. Thus, the poem can be understood to implore people to talk about how black citizens are currently being "crucified." However, a second understanding of the ending is also important. The poem may also suggest that anyone who talks about racism will be figuratively lynched. In other words, churches may deny Christ entrance, but the worse fate befalls those people who broadcast such information in words. The title of the poem actually justifies each reading: the subject of lynching, in the form of domestic terrorism, is "Not for Publication," and those writers who seek to speak about such racism are subject to the figurative lynching of censorship. In either instance, there is presumably grave danger in bringing racism to the attention of others.

The publication date of March 1953 makes Hughes's appearance before HUAC the most immediate context for reading the poem. Does Hughes's poem offer subtle commentary about this event?

Hughes appeared before HUAC on March 26, 1953. His official subpoena to appear before the committee was delivered on March 21 (Rampersad 2: 209). As such, Hughes's poem was already submitted, accepted, in print, and delivered to subscribers by the time Hughes received official word of his impending appearance. However, a growing feeling of his inevitable appearance before the committee had been steadily increasing. For instance, in late October 1951, Hughes's literary agent, Maxim Lieber, left the United States for Mexico in fear of what would happen after he had been linked with the communist activities of Whittaker Chambers (Rampersad 2: 195). Being denounced as a communist before the Senate four years earlier continued to haunt Hughes; his speaking engagements in Fort Worth and San Antonio, Texas, had to be cancelled in early 1952 due to protests against those who sponsored his appearance (Rampersad 2: 197). As 1953 began, there were additional signs that Hughes was bound to be a candidate for McCarthy's witch hunts. NBC cancelled the broadcast of an interview it had taped several months earlier; Hughes's Guggenheim Award had been publicly labeled a "mistake" by the foundation's secretary, and a former member of the National Committee of the Communist Party and editor of the *Daily Worker* identified Hughes as a former Communist Party member (Rampersad 2: 208). By early 1953, Hughes had intensified his attempts to preserve his reputation. When asked by *Ebony* to list the person he admired most, Hughes changed his choice from his childhood idol W.E.B. Du Bois to William Chance as Du Bois was facing up to five years imprisonment for being linked to what was characterized as a publishing outlet of the Soviet Union (Rampersad 2: 209). The imminent threat of Hughes being called before McCarthy's committee had been increasing with each passing month. As his biographer tells us, receiving the subpoena to appear before HUAC had been something Hughes "had been dreading" (Rampersad 2: 209).

Reading the poem in the context of Hughes's pending appearance before HUAC offers several intriguing possibilities for reading the final two lines of "Not for Publication." Is Hughes's statement that "You may be / crucified" (13–14) an uncanny premonition about the kinds of things he would be unable to say before the committee? Is it a reflection of the anxiety Hughes felt about the threat of being called before this committee? Perhaps the phrase "may be" captures the impending doom Hughes anticipates as he reflects upon the inevitable and crucifying experience of appearing before HUAC that he senses is awaiting him. More significantly, the analogy between lynching and crucifixion invokes a means to emotionally communicate both the anticipation and culmination of what was happening to him. It was a means to state verbally what these actions felt like. Only months earlier, the Karamu Theatre in Cleveland had refused to perform Hughes's *Mulatto* "because it ended with a lynching" (Rampersad 2: 199). Now Hughes may have wondered why Americans would instead accept public lynchings where reputations were destroyed.

It is the ambiguous nature of the analogy itself that makes the poem open to such speculation. In fact, at least two other questions come to mind as a result of Hughes's imagery. First, had Hughes not felt the pressures of the nation's anticommunist fervor, what might he have wanted to "talk about"? Second, if Hughes wasn't thinking of himself, who else might he have been thinking about? In other words, in addition to Hughes, who else was being figuratively crucified in America at this time?

The immediate context of the March 1953 publication of Hughes's poem reveals one of the many things about which Hughes might have wanted to talk more freely. Hughes's poetry occupies the final words on page 167 of the March issue of *Crisis*. Though it seems customary to us as contemporary readers, it's important to remember that the ambiguous nature of Hughes's analogy activates a still burgeoning visual literacy among readers as the poem appears within the pages of a magazine filled with photographic images and advertisements. In addition, the first entry on the very next page of the magazine reads:

> *Ingram Appeal*: North Carolina offered a weak argument in support of the six-month suspended sentence imposed on Mack Ingram, the share cropper convicted of "assault by leering" at a white farm girl. . . . Ingram was convicted in November of 1952 and given six months sentence for "assault by leering" at the young woman from a distance of 75 feet. ("Along the N.A.A.C.P. Battlefront" 168)

By the early 1950s, American lynching culture sought to advance the logic that even a black man caught looking in the direction of a white girl had thoughts of rape on his mind. The courtrooms rather than the lynching tree were another forum for warning African Americans about the apparently more civil power of dominant culture. Such court cases also simultaneously sustained the category of whiteness and demonstrated the country's heightened attentiveness and commitment to acting upon information gained through varying modes of surveillance.

Although Hughes did not address the Mack Ingram incident in poetry, he composed one of his longest poems in response to another act of racism also closely associated with lynching. Hughes's "The Ballad of Harry Moore" was circulated only among the Associated Negro Press after Harry Moore; his wife, Harriette; and members of their extended family were killed in Florida on Christmas Eve of 1952 by a bomb that exploded beneath their house. An investigation begun nearly fifty-five years later concluded that four leaders in the local KKK were responsible.[1]

In addition to his previous civil rights work, Harry's actions on behalf of investigating lynchings in the late 1940s drew attention in 1949, when four black men were accused of raping a seventeen-year-old white girl near Orlando. Despite the fact that the girl had actually been beaten by her husband, Charles Greenlee, Sam Shepherd, and Walter Irvin were arrested. The fourth man, Ernest Thomas, managed to escape, only to be shot by a posse a few days later. A mob of five hundred men burned the three men's neighborhood in Groveland when the accused men could not be located and thereby lynched. Though the men were never included among lynching statistics for 1951, Lake County sheriff Willis McCall removed two of the three men from prison. Then, taking justice into his own hands, McCall shot the two men along the side of the road, killing Sam Shepherd and wounding Walter Irvin. Harry Moore's work on behalf of justice became too much for the inflamed local chapter of the KKK to bear.

Just as *Crisis* had reported the incident of Mack Ingram's leering in March 1953, one month later, in its April issue, it published a reflection upon the significance of the death of Harry Moore. A two-page article noted "a shift in the plane of violence from lynching to more sophisticated legal lynching and that new modern instrument of terror,—the hate bomb. The same fears and prejudices motivate . . . bomb-throwers as lynchers" (Cartwright 222). In reaction to the lack of lynchings listed in Tuskegee's statistical reports, the article strongly suggested the institute should "extend their definition of lynching . . . as a technique of racial exploitation,—economic, cultural, and political, to force a choice between subservience or annihilation" (223). The author specifically refers to Sheriff McCall as someone who "staged a one-man lynching" (223).

Expanding the definition of lynching to include the domestic terrorism of bombing reminds us that Hughes's "Ballad of Harry Moore" deserves to be read as an antilynching poem. The fact that lynching had morphed into domestic terrorism and now included bombing and shooting reminds us that the tactics refined during fighting the Axis powers during World War II were now being used to control African Americans. Well after World War II, America, to some degree, continued to be at war with its own citizens. Symbolically, African Americans still rated no better than the fascists, Nazis, or Japanese. More literally, bombing and shooting were the more efficient means of killing.

Hughes's eighty-two-line poem was published in February 1952 in various places by the Associated Negro Press and also set to music in preparation for a March 6, 1952, NAACP fund-raising event to be held at Madison Square Garden (Rampersad 2: 198). Hughes worked out the details for this performance with three musicians including Margaret Bonds (Rampersad 2: 198). Given that the Moores were killed on Christmas Eve, Hughes draws parallels in the poem between the Magi who visited Jesus and the Klansmen who came bearing a bomb. In fact, Hughes's use of the name "Jesus" on three separate occasions in the poem activates the trope of Christ invoked in "Not for Publication." Perhaps Hughes was also referring to this poem in his testimony before HUAC when he spoke of writing "many poems about Christ." It is important to note that no fewer than three of such poems discuss Christ in conjunction with lynching.

Is Hughes suggesting that Moore is one of the people who have been "crucified" for talking about race in the United States? If so, then "Not for Publication" reminds us of Moore and the men he sought to protect. In the poem dedicated to Moore, Hughes extends the notion of crucifixion to suggest that Moore has a voice that calls from his grave to all readers. By portraying him in resurrected form, the same triumph afforded Christ is inscribed on Moore, who overcomes racism. Hughes thus reinstates value upon the dead leader by merging the final narrative of Christ's life with his birth.

Paul Robeson

If Hughes was not thinking about Moore, perhaps he had Paul Robeson in mind when he wrote that talking about racism could lead to a form of figurative crucifixion. Hughes had known and appreciated the artistry of the famous black performer and social protester since at least 1926, when he listened to Robeson singing songs such as "Joshua Fit de Battle" and "Bye and Bye" on his first-ever commercially released records (Duberman 98). In fact, the two knew each other quite well as Robeson spent many years in Harlem when he wasn't traveling the world to sing or perform on stage and in film. By 1936, Robeson had even requested that Hughes provide him some of his poems that might be set to music: Hughes sent him "three about lynching" (Duberman 198). Hughes had also written personal letters to Paul's wife, Essie, and Robeson himself recited two of Hughes's poems from memory before seven thousand people gathered at Mountain Ash, Wales, in 1938 (Duberman 204, 228).

In addition, Robeson met with the poet himself on several occasions as Hughes was very intrigued by the prospect of trying to write various film, radio plays, and dramatic scripts with Robeson in mind in the starring role.[2] On at least two occasions, the two made important public appearances together. Each was featured at the Negro Freedom Rally on June 25, 1944, in Madison Square Garden as well as at a fund-raiser for Henry A. Wallace held in Yankee Stadium before fifty thousand spectators in 1948 (Rampersad 2: 105; 169).

Paul Robeson's biography reads like a depiction of a man who had been politically crucified. Communist paranoia resulted in labeling his activities as falling within a pattern of subversive behavior. Though none of his connections were directly linked to communist political influences, Robeson used Marxist ideals to interrogate the legitimacy of America's claims of freedom and democracy. Much like Hughes, Robeson first became interested in communism during a trip to the USSR in 1934, where he felt "like a human being for the first time since I grew up" (Duberman 190). Paul's son received two years of formal education in the USSR, and Robeson's speech shortly after this first trip on June 24, 1937, at England's Royal Albert Hall, "marked his full emergence as a political spokesman" (Duberman 213).

The parallels between Robeson and Hughes overlap even further before they diverge. By 1943, J. Edgar Hoover inaccurately labeled Robeson "a confidant of high officials of the Party" who was "undoubtedly 100% Communist" (Duberman 280). Together, Hughes and Robeson were denounced in Congress as two of 141 members of the National Citizen's Political Action Committee, which, according to Un-American Activities director J. B. Matthews, constituted "the leading Communist front organization in the United States" (Rampersad 2: 90). Congress successfully created a fetish in its battle against black political activists by labeling them red. This fetishization conveniently paralleled the fact that the American branch of the Communist Party had doubled its membership in Harlem by adding four hundred new members during a three-month span in 1944 (Duberman 284).

Robeson's and Hughes's reactions to red-baiting, FBI surveillance, and cancelled public appearances soon diverged as Robeson intensified his stance and Hughes gradually withdrew. Interestingly, Robeson spoke for communism less often than he spoke against racism in its most visual form of lynching. With fifty-six blacks dying between June 1945 and September 1956 as a result of various acts of domestic terrorism, Robeson used a speaking opportunity at a September 12, 1946, rally in Madison Square Garden to denounce lynching: "This swelling wave of lynch murders and mob assaults . . . represents the ultimate limit of bestial brutality. . . . [S]*top the lynchers!* What about it, President Truman? Why have you failed to speak out against this evil?" (Duberman 305). Perhaps Robeson's financial standing as a result of his highly successful stints as a performer quite literally afforded him the courage to continue speaking out against racism and lynching. As we have seen, Hughes responded by turning to a more covert mode of resistance.

Robeson's use of communist ideas was often aimed at eliminating lynching. He joined with W.E.B. Du Bois and others in 1946 to push for yet another attempt at an antilynch law, which culminated in a private meeting between Robeson and President Truman in the Oval Office (Duberman 307). Lynching became an even deeper personal issue for Robeson when he was invited to perform in Peekskill, New York, on August 27, 1949. When the group sponsoring Robeson's appearance was labeled as a front for a communist organization located in California, the ensuing newspaper headlines reported the results: "Lynch Mob Runs Amuck at Robeson's Concert" (Duberman 366). Met by burning crosses and a full-blown riot, Robeson was rushed out of town and back to New York City. Defiantly, Robeson rescheduled the concert for the very next week, where he was met by guards to protect him, eight thousand protesters bent on intimidating him, and two life-size images of himself being hung from a rope. With his life at stake, Robeson heard threats that "We'll kill you!" and security patrols removed two men who were wielding high-powered rifles within range of Robeson's makeshift stage (Duberman 369). Robeson was whisked away immediately in a car while sprawled lengthwise "on the rear floor, while two of the trade-union bodyguards covered him with their bodies" (Duberman 369). Immediately after, another riot occurred at this September 4 appearance, just as it had a week earlier.

In attempting to gain the rights afforded many white citizens, the black Robeson had called upon the social philosophy of communist thought. The result: Robeson was now a target of double intensity as he was coded both black and red. Interestingly enough, the punishment for a man coded both black and red was the same for a man who was simply coded black. In fact, dominant culture relied upon the power of American lynching culture to curb such behavior. In one inflection, American lynching culture turned to the same mode of control for silencing "reds" as it had previously used to silence blacks. Apparently the greatest intimidation America could muster against a "red" was to implement what had been used and refined by American lynching culture.

Hence, in the week following Robeson's Peekskill concert, the KKK received 722 letters of application from citizens throughout the surrounding county of Westchester (Duberman 697). Moreover, the intimidation initiated at Peekskill was mimicked and extended at other places around the country. Residents of Tallahassee, Florida, and Birmingham, Alabama, not only tied images of Robeson to trees but went so far as to literally set these effigies on fire (Duberman 374). Faced with uncertainty about what should be done to a black communist, Americans called upon the logic of lynching as a means of emotional release and intimidation. Robeson's links to communism allowed them an opportunity to treat him as yet another black man it needed to lynch. In fact, treating a black civil rights leader this way illustrated that such allegations of communism were mere window dressing for suppressing the same access to justice that American lynching culture had been assertively denying blacks since at least the 1890s.

Later, in 1950, Robeson would have his passport revoked. Although certainly Robeson's links to communism brought great scrutiny, the loss of his right to travel came in no small measure as a response to his passionate verbal rants against lynching. In June 1950, Robeson spoke in Chicago before the National Labor Conference for Negro Rights. True to the logic of his dual perspectives on Marxist reasoning and racial prejudice, Robeson linked the violence of lynching with economic struggles. In the minds of some who were living in the 1950s, the two were very much related. Rather than save the world from the communist menace, Robeson implored his listeners:

> Ask the Negro ministers in Birmingham whose homes were bombed by the Ku Klux Klan what is the greatest menace in their lives. . . . Ask Willie McGee, languishing in a Mississippi prison. . . . Ask Haywood Patterson, somewhere in America, a fugitive from Alabama barbarism for a crime he, nor any of the Scottsboro boys, ever committed. Ask the growing numbers of Negro unemployed in Chicago and Detroit. Ask the fearsome lines of relief clients in Harlem. . . . Ask fifteen million American Negroes, if you please, "What is the greatest menace in your lives?" and they will answer in a thunderous voice, "Jim-Crow Justice! Mob Rule!

Segregation! Job Discrimination!" in short—White Supremacy and all its vile works. Our enemies are the lynchers, the profiteers. (Duberman 387)

Robeson's comments collapsed the distance between lynchers and profiteers, suggesting that the two groups were essentially the same. Only one month after linking the two, Robeson's passport was confiscated and withheld for the next eight years. What might have happened to Hughes had he made such an overt statement?

Like Hughes, Robeson's figurative crucifixion began well before his official appearance before HUAC in 1957. Robeson seemed to demand that this crucifixion intensify when he made the choice to present the document *We Charge Genocide* in New York before the United Nations on December 18, 1951. The petition invoked the term "genocide" to evoke the shock and sensationalism associated with the trials of Nazi officials held in Nuremberg. The petition documented all forms of lynching including the recent cases of Willie McGee, the Martinsville Seven, and the Trenton Six. It is interesting to note that this statement appeared only months after Hughes published *Montage*, which featured the poem "Dream Deferred." *We Charge Genocide* offered these varying forms of oppression as evidence that expanded the traditional definition of "genocide" from "mass murder" to include bodily, mental, or economic harm: "high infant mortality rates among blacks, widespread disenfranchisement, malnutrition, a lack of medical and health services, denial of fair employment and educational opportunities, segregation in public accommodations, urban ghettoes, mob violence and police brutality, as well as a tradition of bias in the courts and prison system" (Dray 410). In addition to this list, the document directly addressed lynching directly and by extending its definition:

> There was a time when racist violence had its center in the South. . . . Once most of the violence against Negroes occurred in the countryside. . . . Now there is not a great American city from New York to Cleveland, or Detroit . . . from New Orleans to Los Angeles, that is not disgraced by the wanton killing of innocent Negroes. . . .
>
> Once the classic method of lynching was the rope. Now it is the policeman's bullet. . . . But by far the majority of Negro murders are never recorded. . . . [B]odies . . . often horribly mutilated, are found in the woods or washed up on the shore of a river or lake. This is a well-known pattern of American culture. . . . Mass murder

on the basis of race is a powerful source of constant terror, as it is intended to be, to the whole Negro people. As a result of the pattern of extra-legal violence in which they live out their lives, if they do live, the entire Negro people exists in a constant fear that cannot fail to cause serious bodily and mental harm. . . .

Perennial, hour by hour, moment by moment lynching of the Negro's soul in countless psychological, in myriad physical forms, that is the greatest and most enduring lynching of all. This is written into the spiritual hanging of all those millions, it is carved into the daily thinking, woven into their total living experience. (Civil Rights Congress 9)

As evidence of their greatest grievance, the only photograph that accompanied the published form of the statement documented the lynching of Dooley Morton and Bert Moore in Columbus, Mississippi.

Robeson personally delivered this petition in New York, and William Patterson appeared simultaneously in Paris before the UN General Assembly. Interestingly enough, Hughes's relationship with William and Louise Patterson "epitomized his dilemma as an artist who loved the left but dared not speak, out of fear that his tongue might be cut out altogether. Repeatedly he solicited their opinions, obviously valued them, but could not, or would not, bring himself to follow them" (Rampersad 2: 93). In fact, Hughes's 1942 collection of poems *Shakespeare in Harlem* was dedicated to Louise Patterson.

Hughes's public responses to the treatment of Robeson varied between silence and anger. During 1950, "although he may have felt outrage at the official harassment of Robeson, especially the restrictions on his travel overseas, he declined to join any protest" (Rampersad 2: 181). However, six years later Hughes more than hinted at his personal attitude when, in an article for the *Defender*, he took issue with America's double standard. When William Faulkner asserted that he would willingly "take up arms against the Federal government," Hughes sarcastically wondered if Faulkner would have his passport revoked just as Robeson had for making much less volatile statements (Rampersad 2: 352).

The example made of Paul Robeson demonstrates that the opportunity for ending lynching via the logic of Marxist thought was effectively silenced. America redoubled its position against racist violence by coupling the discrimination of blacks with the fear of communism. The interrogation of American racism by means of Marxist thought was effectively coupled with the threat of USSR infiltration. For many Americans, the only thing as bad as being black was being red: in their eyes, Robeson and Hughes were both. Mack Ingram and Harry Moore were black, but Paul Robeson and Langston Hughes were considered double threats. As such, this "late period of Hughes's work provides a special opportunity to revisit the historic tensions, divergences, and convergences between the 'black' and the 'red'" (Kim 435).

In regard to "Not for Publication," the issue is not so much to decide whether Hughes had either Harry Moore, Paul Robeson, or himself in mind when he suggested that there were those who would be crucified for speaking about racism in America. Instead, the historical context of this poem highlights the fact that Hughes's pronoun "you" can be applied to many people. This short list could easily be expanded.

In short, too many people were figuratively crucified for attempting to highlight the issue of persistent and evolving racism. Hughes's poem successfully captures this cultural reality by using crucifixion as an analogy for lynching to collapse the distance between racial violence and censorship. "Not for Publication" was particularly appropriate for 1953 even though no official lynchings were recorded during the entire year.

La Poésie Negro-Americaine

"Dream Deferred" is a poem with which many readers are familiar. Placing it in discussion alongside "Not for Publication" is extremely warranted. Briefly tabling its typical 1951 context, I want to begin to defamiliarize reader assumptions about this poem and explore the possibility of an alternative reading by considering the later, 1966, appearance of this poem. "Dream Deferred" appeared in other publications after its 1951 appearance in *Montage*. The placement of this poem in one of these collections further highlights the need to consider Hughes's use of analogy. Hughes served as sole editor of a bilingual edition of poems written by black Americans. Issued in 1966, *La Poésie Negro-Americaine* featured poems printed in both French and English. Intending the collection primarily for a French audience, Hughes included two poems by other poets with lynching overtones: Claude McKay's "If We Must Die," and Countee Cullen's "Christ Recrucified." He also included nine of his own poems.

The sequencing in the presentation of poems was always very important to Hughes. After *Montage*, this importance only intensified. Even later, in 1967, this poem's placement in *The Panther and the Lash* creates points of contact with lynching as the subject is addressed in a poem that immediately follows "Dream Deferred" (this connection is discussed further in the conclusion). The sequence between Hughes's third and fourth poems in his 1966 bilingual anthology is equally striking. "Dream Deferred" (still titled "Harlem") appears immediately after "Not for Publication." As such, the last image in readers' minds before reading "Dream Deferred" is that of crucifixion. This particular edition offers an intertextual sequencing where the connection between crucifixion and Hughes's imagery in "Dream Deferred" guides reader interpretation in a surprising new direction. For the readers of Hughes's 1966 sequence, the imagery in "Dream Deferred" would have had an opportunity to suggest that Hughes addressed racism by showing that dreams could also be figuratively crucified. In this overseas context, Hughes could afford to be more direct and overt in 1966. In fact, this overseas edition offers a fresh glance into Hughes's strikingly complex poem. It is this later context that becomes a new point of entry into what Hughes may have been doing in 1951.

Understandably, "Dream Deferred" presents the most challenging and complex consideration of Hughes's engagement with American lynching culture. As we have seen, Hughes functioned under intense censorship during the era in which the poem was first published in 1951. There was little change for Hughes in regard to what he could say in mainstream sources between 1951 and 1953. The poem's highly elusive imagery, coupled with Hughes's inability to "talk" about lynching during a time when he was negotiating censorship raises an intriguing consideration: Is Hughes using lynching as an analogy in "Dream Deferred" as he did in "Not for Publication"? Does this 1966 appearance suggest that he was showing through images what he could not say in words in 1951? If so, is it reasonable to consider that having one's hopes deferred might feel like having your dreams lynched? Had America found a means to lynch Harlem's hopes by perpetually delaying their fulfillment?

It is the interplay between Hughes's emerging use of analogy, the political constraints of censorship, Hughes's own choice in regard to sequencing this poem in concert with "Not for Publication," the expanded meaning of the term "lynching," the historical connection between food and lynching, and the refined complexity of Hughes's artistic engagement with photography that justifies this ambitious reconsideration of Hughes's poem within the context of lynching. Elusiveness itself is inherent (and thus possibly intentional) in a poem that questions everything and asserts nothing. It is inevitable that any rereading of this poem explore and consider rather than find and know. One of the first things we note in any context is that Hughes's poem reads as if it circles from one bright image to another, like photographic images being projected from a slide-show carousel.

Photography

While Hughes engaged in multiple art mediums beyond the written page including music, drama, film, and various visual arts, his application of photographic principles became even more refined when he was first composing the poem for publication in *Montage* in 1951. His personal associations with photographers were extensive. In fact, as early as 1934 he spent extended time with Henri Cartier-Bresson, widely regarded as the most important documentary photojournalist of the era.[3] Hughes also worked with his former student at Atlanta University, photographer Griffith J. Davis. For *Ebony*, they collaborated on three different photojournalistic articles, two about a Harlem church and Harlem entertainers, and another on Atlanta's tenements and artistic culture.[4] Each of these articles was written at the same time that Hughes was finalizing his draft of *Montage* featuring the poem "Dream Deferred."

Hughes's most public links with photography came later in 1955, when he teamed with Roy DeCarava on *The Sweet Flypaper of Life* and, in 1956, with Milton Meltzer on *A Pictorial History of the Negro in America*. While Hughes's montage technique and collage aesthetic are important lenses for understanding his other extended works, the realm of photography is the most relevant to Hughes's technique as employed within an individual poem such as "Dream Deferred."

Hughes was actively engaged with the world of photography from 1948 to 1951. Surrounded by some of its most innovative and celebrated practitioners, Hughes became invested in creating a photo-text of Harlem. Hughes pitched this idea complete "down to page layouts, and specific photo choices" to a photographer for the project he titled "Ups and Downs" in 1950 (Blair 54). Such an ambitious project serves as an illuminating context as *Montage* was being drafted, revised, and published during this time. An understanding of Hughes's engagement with photography excites our consideration of how this medium helps us understand "Dream Deferred."

Sara Blair's reading of Harlem's postwar literary texts asserts that much of the power of the photograph comes through its ability to serve as an analogy. She has found that a work like Ralph Ellison's *Invisible Man* is a text that "suppresses its own visual informing referents" (xx). Through photography, Harlem became a place in which writers "inaugurated an alternative vector of documentary imaging, site-specific and self-conscious to which a host of writers attuned" (Blair xix). Given that Ellison was an established photographer and close friend to Hughes, it is interesting to consider how much Ellison's interest in photography earned him the book dedication he received from Hughes in *Montage*.

Marion Palfi

Among the various photographers Hughes worked with during this era, Marion Palfi deserves extra attention. Palfi met Hughes shortly after her arrival in America while she was working on her first photographic study of minority artists. Born in Berlin, she fled Nazi Germany and arrived in the United States in 1940. Hughes immediately became one of "her most ardent supporters" (Lindquist-Cock 6). Consistent with the testimony of those who knew Hughes well, Palfi referred to him as "among her 'dearest friends' and her most important 'guide'" (Blair 54). Hughes might have felt a good deal of camaraderie with Palfi as she, too, was mostly self-supported, even sometimes "pawning personal items" just to pay for the expenses of a project she felt was important (Palfi, "The South").[5]

Hughes knew Palfi's work intimately. He had invited her to speak to one of the classes he taught at Atlanta University in 1947 (Rampersad 2: 128). As we might imagine, these classroom visits were quite routine for Palfi, who frequently showed "hundreds of slides documenting injustices" (Lindquist-Cock 5). From 1946 to 1949, Palfi was taking pictures of children in "Florida shantytowns, in reformatories and jails, California migrant camps, and the irony of the poverty in the power center of Washington D.C." (Lindquist-Cock 7). These images later appeared in various schools and libraries around the country under the title *Children in America* and then were published in 1952 under the title *Suffer Little Children*. One of Hughes's quotes was even used as a caption to a photo in the series taken between 1946 and 1949: "A Palfi photograph brings us face to face with hidden realties that its surface only causes us to begin to explore" (Palfi, plate 13). Palfi's work is important because the timing of Hughes's greatest interaction with her coincides with the time he was drafting and revising "Dream Deferred."

It is interesting to consider how Palfi's work may have influenced Hughes's approach to poetry. The similar attitudes of the two about their subject matter would have made such influence highly possible and reciprocal. Like Hughes, Palfi was "deeply emotional about the suffering of humanity in many forms" (Enyeart 3). Moreover, she responded to being "unexpectedly confronted with the fact that the United States was not the ideal society many envisioned" by immediately becoming "involved in the struggles of minorities for social justice" (Lindquist-Cock 5). Her attitude was further demonstrated in one of the captions she wrote for a photograph taken in New York City that was published in *Suffer Little Children*: "it's like the murdering of little angels" (Palfi, plate 4). Like Hughes's "Dream Deferred," she did not seek the "dramatic moment" in her photos, but instead captured the "ongoing existence of suffering, pain, and frustrated need" (Lindquist-Cock 11).

Documenting city life was clearly a popular organizational principle for both the poet and photographer. Both Hughes and Palfi had ideas for such projects, and their timing was nothing short of uncanny. In fact, when Hughes wanted a photographer in 1950 for his aforementioned project on Harlem titled "Ups and Downs," he sought out Palfi. A year later, Palfi began a project that became titled "In These Ten Cities" as she recorded the racial discord, financial plight, and overall misery of people in cities such as Detroit and Phoenix. Later that same year, Hughes issued *Montage* as his own retrospective on Harlem's ups and downs, and the original title of this poem as "Harlem" becomes even more significant.

Equally important, Palfi, like Hughes, responded to American lynching culture. Her 1949 study *There Is No More Time* was conducted in Irwinton, Georgia, in response to the lynching of Caleb Hill. Hill was arrested on disorderly conduct charges on the night of May 30, 1949, and was reported to be drunk. The twenty-eight-year-old chalk-mine worker was removed from prison the same night—when Sheriff George Hatcher purposefully allowed two white men to claim the keys to the jail cell and speed away with Hill. Hill's beaten body was found on the side of the road with a bullet in his head and another through his chest. Two men were later brought in on charges and then, in typical fashion,

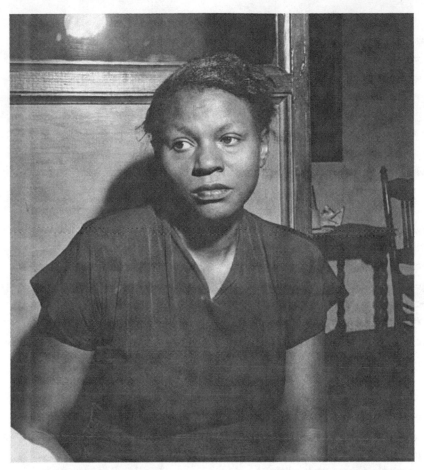

Fig. 3.2. *Wife of a Lynch Victim, Irwinton, Georgia,* 1949. Photograph by Marion Palfi. By permission of Collection Center for Creative Photography, University of Arizona © 1998 Arizona Board of Regents.

released because of insufficient evidence when no one would testify against them. Among the men who could have testified was a black man who occupied the jail cell with Hill that evening; however, he was apparently so badly intimidated, threatened, and terrified that doing so would have likely cost him his life. The lynching was front-page news in the *New York Times* for the entire next week. Furthermore, Palfi spent two full months in Irwinton taking photographs of several citizens in town. Near the end of her visit, she risked her own life to get a chance to meet the victim's wife. Palfi's profoundly moving still image of this encounter, *Wife of a Lynch Victim, Irwinton, Georgia,* is perhaps her best-known photograph (fig. 3.2).

Reading Palfi's two most well-known images reveals overlapping parallels with "Dream Deferred" in regard to technique. Hughes would have known each of these images personally. Palfi's *Wife of a Lynch Victim* reminds viewers of the importance of considering lynching's survivors—those people who are forced to live in the shadow of lynching in its various forms. In this image, lynching does not seem to end so much as to linger. The face of Caleb's wife sustains equal parts shock, loss, acceptance, and silence as long as two months after her husband's death. In fact, the image communicates much more than her words that accompanied the image: "Caleb was a good man . . . he believed in his rights and therefore he died" (Palfi, plate 40). Hughes's engagement with photography was substantial, and his exposure to Palfi's images predates his publication of "Dream Deferred" and "Not for Publication." He believed that photographs "comment upon the social order that creates" the imaged lives.[6] As a result, the picture prods viewers to wonder about the society of Georgia, which can oppress not only its victims, but also its survivors. This image also reminds us of the need to conceal anger. Here, the wife's face portrays an outward acceptance that perhaps masks her inner frustration.

Unlike the pure documentation mode intensified by the accessibility of smaller hand-held cameras that seemingly found rather than orchestrated their subject matter, this image is staged in the remote darkness of a home still resonating with the absence of the woman's husband. It is only the artist, symbolized in the photo via the remaining camera lighting that reflects back in the mirror above her head that enables the viewer to question the significance of this imagery. Such reminders of the intentional staging suggest the lengths to which Palfi went to secure this image. The artist is purposefully present in the analogy rather than intentionally distant in the presentation of the image.

This lighting, with its overtones of police interrogation, reverses the fields of victim and criminal. Viewers want information that the victim longs to withhold. Worst of all, this interrogation supplants the real police investigation that never happened. Hill's wife, not the lynchers, is figuratively arrested. The victim is prosecuted, refusing or unable to speak, and the photographer and viewer are linked as the only known entities willing to invest their energy in collecting evidence. In differing degrees, the subject of the photograph, the photographer, and the viewer must cope with anger. Such anger is also paramount to Hughes's poetic project *Montage of a Dream Deferred*, where "the concealment of anger becomes the dominant mode of the sequence" (Smethurst 160).

As a result, viewers are made to acknowledge and question their own presence as an observer. To what degree are they, too, guilty of prosecuting the victim rather than those who committed the murder? The interpretive mode of questioning is itself another parallel between Palfi's work and that of Hughes's "Dream Deferred." The repeated questions issued by the speaker in Hughes's poem mirror the words of George Berkowitz, who commented on Palfi's photographs by stating: "they do not accuse as much as they question" (1). Perhaps one significant testament to the influence of photography on Hughes's poem rests in its successive questioning. The meanings that the viewers are called on to discover from looking at photographs or reading poems remain elusive and irreducible because analogies are inherently unstable. But viewers keep looking because this uncertainty is countered by the rewards of colliding dissimilar ideas in such a startling way that the connections linger.

It is possible to read Palfi's second-most popular photograph, *In the Shadow of the Capitol, Washington D.C.*, as an image that visualizes the realities of having one's dreams deferred in Washington, D.C. (fig. 3.3). The Capitol Building in the background becomes symbolic of the dream of institutionalized democracy, and the broken scooter and unhappy children are things that, like the items mentioned in Hughes's poem, were once good but have now gone bad. Reading the photograph as an analogy suggests that the dream is within the interpretive reach of the viewer, but impossible for the residents of this neighborhood to grasp. The tension between their existence and this visual icon highlights the frustrations of the viewer while simultaneously highlighting the long-held acceptance of these children. But the image, as an analogy, celebrates ambiguity. Have the children turned their back on political democracy in search of help from the artist (who appears to them unseen in the form of the real photographer taking the picture) or the viewer who may care enough to help these suffering children? In this way, we wonder if the child in front is leaning forward in such a way as to suggest if the photographer can be of help in any way.

Reading "Dream Deferred" through the dual lenses of censorship and photography reminds us that the genre of photography, so paramount in the American cultural practice of documenting lynchings, might be understood to have some of its own strategies invoked by Hughes as

Fig. 3.3. *In the Shadow of the Capitol, Washington, D.C.*, 1946–48. Photograph by Marion Palfi. By permission of Collection Center for Creative Photography, University of Arizona © 1998 Arizona Board of Regents.

a means to attempt to signify on the genre itself. In such a climate, Hughes possessed the artistic strategies of photography at his full command. We wonder if Hughes embraced this ambiguity as he uncovered the reality that talking (as stated in "Not for Publication") could not pass. To resist considering that Hughes's images could function in preciously this way only retrenches some of the literary perceptions that Hughes's poems lack depth and artistic complexity.

Lynched Dreams

Why might Hughes suggest that dreams are figuratively lynched in Harlem? Perhaps he would do this in order to communicate that Harlem's citizens still harbor memories of lynching within them. Earlier in *Montage*, Hughes alludes to such memories in unmistakable fashion. "Not a Movie" records the cultural history of a man who has been hit in the head and whipped as a result of trying to vote. The man's response was to elude the Klan by getting on the late-night train and staying on it all the way until it arrives in Harlem. Certainly such fear has not been forgotten simply because he now lives in Harlem. In "Dream Deferred," lynching may be one of the means to activate the memory of the most painful of southern experiences to reinscribe the power of socioeconomic disappointment felt by blacks in the North.

Food

In considering if Hughes used food as a vehicle that was safely distanced and yet highly suggestive of lynching, it is important to note that cultural connections between food and lynching were very common. It is no small matter that food, in the form of "strange fruit," became the preferred vehicle of the most powerful metaphoric statement ever made on lynching. This metaphor resulted in part from the language used in newspaper reports, which often featured headlines that read "Colored Man Roasted Alive," and public burnings of blacks were commonly referred to as a "Negro Barbeque" (Apel 23). Other terms with overtones to eating include referring to lynchings as "coon cooking, and main fare" (Allen 175).

Despite the fact that such derogatory metaphors were most often invoked by the dominant culture to dehumanize black victims, Hughes himself actually linked the two realms on at least two occasions before the 1951 publication of "Dream Deferred." As early as 1922, he spoke of lynching in his poem "The South." Here, he referenced the act of souveniring as seen in the descriptive images of searching through the charred remains of fire for the victim's bones. However, this reference in "The South" illuminates not so much the practice of souveniring as the lynching metaphor of eating. This can be seen clearly in the second line of the poem, in which the act of "eating" has left behind its red juices on the participant's mouth. More recently, Hughes reminded readers of "Comment" (1946) that encounters with the natural world's predators were not so nearly as deadly as interacting with human beings who practice lynching. In the final stanza, Hughes suggests people can be killed (lynched) to become the main (meat) ingredient in a soup.

Hughes's references after 1951 increase the likelihood that food and lynching are related in "Dream Deferred." After 1951, Hughes made two unmistakable references to food in the context of lynching. Although Billie Holiday's rendition of Abel Meeropol's poem "Strange Fruit" was first popularized seventeen years earlier, it was still fresh in Hughes's mind when he wrote his opera *Esther* in 1956. Hughes can not resist portraying the character Haman in the context of lynching culture. As a result, Hughes has Haman speak these lines as he revels in the idea of hanging Mordecai from the gallows:

> Let his eyes be eyes
> For the crows to pluck
> And his lips be lips
> For the wind to suck. (*CW* 6: 123)

Hughes plays off of lines 9–10 of Holiday's song by rhyming "pluck" with "suck" and by specifically citing the imagery of "crow" and "wind," which are mentioned in these same lines of the song as well. Evidently the connection between lynching and food was so ingrained in Hughes through his knowledge of Holiday's song that he clearly alluded to it long after its release.

Was Hughes also subtly invoking the memory of this song in "Dream Deferred"? In transmitting his complaint, does Hughes portray the dreams of the present by returning to the memories of the past? Where Holiday sang in her final stanza of fruit that the sun would rot, Hughes's first image in the poem more specifically supplies readers with what the sun does to a raisin. "Strange Fruit" described the eyes that bulge after a man has been lynched, and Hughes ends his poem by suggesting an explosion. In line 8 of her song, Holiday sang of the scent of burnt flesh; Hughes wonders about the stink of rotten meat.

Finally, Hughes's 1962 history of the NAACP refers to the metaphor of food as he recounts the coverage of a lynching he knew all too well. Within a full-paragraph summary of the lynching of Jesse Washington, Hughes writes in his own words: "Innumerable photographs were taken of the gruesome spectacle. . . . [The] findings concerning this human barbeque were published in a special 8-page supplement to *Crisis* entitled 'The Waco Horror'" (*CW* 10: 51). Hughes connected food with lynching in very sophisticated ways on at least four separate occasions in his writings.

How does Hughes use food imagery throughout *Montage*? In addition to the references to food in "Dream Deferred," *Montage* uses food imagery on three other occasions. It seems highly significant that each of these references to food is made in reference to people. Hughes's poem "Mellow" suggests that white women can be seen with the popular and famous black men in Harlem. These women are compared to plums. They fall from a tree located beyond what is described as a fence or barrier intent on killing any who overstep its boundaries. The message is clear: the myth of black men pursuing white women is being undermined. Rather than black men aggressively advancing toward such women, the white women pursue the men in Harlem. Though not directly stated, the desirability, not the fear, of the male black body is reinscribed. Although blacks were once subject to being lynched in the South, this northern landscape offers moments of topophilia as a site where African Americans can not only experience what was once forbidden fruit, but also escape the topophobia associated with the literal threat of being lynched.

The poem "125th Street" offers three different food-related images of the human face. The human face is significant as it offers the outside world a "fluid continuum of" black identify (Julien 255). Hughes's poem reveals that this identity is simultaneously projected and hidden. The poem reminds us that, to the outside world, the black face is nearly unreadable because it is so ambiguous; hence, it lends itself well to the same strokes of visual imagery that photography can reproduce. First likened to a chocolate bar, a face in this poem appears to be sweet and waiting to be consumed. Compared to the smile of a jack-o-lantern, another face is bright at first sight but also potentially filled with a burning anger, as if a flame has been lit inside. Finally, another face offers a grin so broad it is compared to a sliced section of melon; but is it sincerely happy, or does it only look that way? After all, it has been cut. Such ambiguity remains unresolved as these facial projections function in a similar manner to photographic analogies, veiling as much as they reveal.

Given Hughes's use of imagery, these faces counter the idea of the human body being portrayed as food waiting to be consumed. These are faces that deserve interpersonal contemplation. Where such strange fruit was once a metaphor to explore the notion of lynching, here Hughes offers these faces a complexity that undermines their apparent simplicity. In fact, they do not represent people who are merely alive and inviting. They may also be cautious of being consumed and cast aside as food, conceal a deep rage and fiery anger, and mask a painful past covered with a persona that is seen to be laughing and smiling outwardly.

In seeing New York City as a place of similar integration and complex interdependence, the final poem of *Montage* portrays the relationship between Harlem and the rest of Manhattan through food imagery. "Island" offers the final vision of this relationship as New York City is referred to as a "Chocolate-custard / Pie of a town" (7–8). Harlem's chocolate citizens are surrounded by white (or yellow "custard") people. This all-American pie is not apple, but an integrated dual flavor. Is Hughes being a realist, suggesting the fact that as close as these two racial realms are, they are still very distinct parts? Or is he dreaming again that although this separation is distinct now, its reconciliation is only deferred, not permanent? As a revision to American lynching culture, perhaps this image of an integrated pie is intended to counter the commonplace notion of regarding America as a melting pot. Ideally, such citizens are both independently distinct, and even better when combined together. Like so many other poems in this collection, "Island" communicates through ambiguity.

Dream Deferred

It is uncanny how much Hughes's imagery resembles the lynched body. Looking at images of lynched bodies makes this surprising connection especially clear. Lynching may be an appropriate analogy for conveying how a Harlem citizen could feel after having their dreams deferred. Given Hughes's need to negotiate censorship, it would not be surprising if he used analogy to allude to the plight of those living in 1950s Harlem.

Under the constraints of such censorship, Hughes's analogy would have to be ambiguous. He would have to show rather than tell.

It is not hard to imagine the images in "Dream Deferred" in relationship to lynching victims. The first vehicle Hughes uses in the poem is that of a raisin in the sun. Hughes tells us that these dreams are not a grape that dries up but an already dried raisin that becomes even drier. It is not difficult to liken this image to a black body wrinkling in the sun after being burned.

Because lynch victims were often tortured in sadistic fashion for extended hours before their public executions, they would also develop open wounds. Hughes's second image in the poem is that of a sore that festers and runs. Such lesions could result from absorbing the lashes from strips of thin tree branches, chains, or a whip. The smell of burnt flesh is unforgettable, and Hughes next wonders if unfulfilled dreams "stink like rotten meat" (6). Hughes's image furthers the connections between the body and a piece of meat. Historically, lynch victims were discussed and labeled as if they were the main course for some perverse feast. Hughes's idea that dreams can "crust and sugar over / like a syrupy sweet," (7–8) continues the association of what happens when the human body is exposed to heat.

We should remember that dreams cannot dry up, stink, or crust over, but human bodies can. The victim who gets hung sags from the tree looking like something heavy to carry. Moreover, lynched bodies bloat when they are left at the dark bottom of a river bed, and human eyes literally explode when overexposed to heat as in "Strange Fruit." Descriptions of Sam Hose's eyes exploding serve as a disturbing reminder of this fact. All that was once good or had the potential to be good has now gone bad. The raisin is now too dry to eat; the sore that could heal has festered too long; the meat that was once prime is now rotten; the dessert once so appealing has been overexposed to heat to run beyond its dish to blacken the rim. In each of these instances, Hughes shows rather than tells.

The reality of the North rests not only in the fact that many of its citizens bring with them the memory of lynching from the South, but also in the fact that the North has also found another way to figuratively lynch dreams. As Hughes's poetry has demonstrated, there are several ways to be lynched. One can be lynched literally, figuratively through imprisonment, personally through being accused as a communist or testifying before HUAC, or artistically through censorship. The body, of course, can literally be lynched. But on the figurative level, mobility, public image, and poetry can be, too. Dominant culture was in a transition in regard to how to successfully exert power in postwar America. It was moving toward a hegemony that distanced its interests from those it sought to oppress. By inflicting "nonlethal assaults," this culture had uncovered "more than one way to deny African Americans their rights as citizens" thus "there was less reason for whites in the North or South to resort to lynching as a means to dominate black people" (Goldsby 289). Nonetheless, these assaults and denials had many of the same effects on its victims as lynching. The poem may attempt to capture how it feels to have to wait for full integration and equality. Metaphorically, it is as painful as having one's hopes lynched.

Montage of a Dream Deferred

It is also important to understand the literary context in which "Dream Deferred" first appeared. "Dream Deferred" became the signature poem in the very complex sequence titled *Montage of a Dream Deferred* (1951). In addition to veiling the influence of past pain on modern art, *Montage* also documents Hughes's highest aspirations. Artistically, *Montage's* aspirations can be regarded as attempting to enable the process of reading to serve as a rehearsal for the soon-to-be and much anticipated performance of social integration. As such, the sequence symbolizes the advantages of desegregating as each poem conveys its greatest resonance from its collective intertextuality. It is also precisely how a collection of well-ordered photographs communicates its meanings. To read the sequence, many small poems must be unified through the process of integrating each of the individual ideas written on white pages in black letters. This organizing principle of *Montage* suggests that reading is an integrative process that holds the so-long-hoped-for capacity to form a whole out of disparate parts. With the term "deferred," Hughes suggests that the dream of successful integration has not suffered outright rejection so much as its realization is being unduly and agonizingly postponed.

In the final poem of *Montage*, Hughes extends the thematic imagery introduced earlier in "Theme for English B," where Hughes envisioned the response by a native North Carolinian to his teacher's request to write an essay. Near the end of "Theme for English B," the speaker envisions that his community might be as integrated as the black letters on the white pages of his essay: together and distinct, yet completely dependant upon each other. In this way, *Montage* models the idea that the sublime insight and illumination that occur on the interpretive level of reading can mirror the exhilaration synonymous with the fulfillment of the dream of integrating human beings socially. The delay of this integration is perhaps one of the realities that has led to the lynching of Harlem's dreams.

Bop

As a whole, *Montage* also contains several subtle elements of violence. The concept of "Be-Bop" that Hughes explores throughout *Montage* highlights both the transition of Harlem and the violence underscoring its music. The concept of bebop is referenced twice in the epigraph to the collection, and it appears in several places throughout the sequence. Hughes defines bop's connection to violence in his contemporaneous November 19, 1949, newspaper column featuring his character Jesse Simple. Numerous "Simple columns" appeared in the *Chicago Defender* beginning in 1942 before becoming so noteworthy that they later were collected and expanded in various works by Hughes. In this column, Simple explains to Boyd a very significant difference between "Re-Bop" and "Be-Bop": "Re-Bop was an imitation like most of the white boys play. Be-Bop is the real thing like the colored boys play" (*CW* 7: 227). Equally important, Simple explains that the music "comes out of them dark days. . . . Folks who ain't suffered much cannot play Bop, neither appreciate it" (*CW* 7: 228). It is not formed from simple depression however, but rather out of physical violence. Boyd is told that it comes specifically from sounds which are "beaten right out of some Negro's head" (*CW* 7: 228). He refers to this specific form of violence no fewer than three times in this short piece.

Simple emphatically suggests that "Be-Bop" is so complex that "white folks don't know what they are singing about, even yet." Said another way, bop communicates through the practice of transcoding, in which "narratives of love and loss systematically transcode other forms of yearning and mourning associated with histories of dispersal and exile and the remembrance of unspeakable terror" (Gilroy 201).

Hughes refers to something other than "Be-Bop" or "Re-Bop" throughout *Montage*. On four occasions, he uses the phrase "De-Dop." Is Hughes simply creating a term that rhymes with "Be-Bop," or is he using the first two letters of "*deferred*" to suggest yet another form of music that has its roots in the realization that dreams have been deferred? If perhaps "De-Dop" is a means of adding a further level of depth to bop, it might suggest the joyful music formed from delay. If "Be-Bop" was born of the dark days of violence, and "Re-Bop" captures the level of dominant culture's all-too-successful appropriation of it, then "De-Dop" is the new jazzlike variation of an old song where syncopation is more than a mode of delivery: it is the symbolic response of a deeply internalized reality. It is not difficult to hesitate in delivering lines 25 and 30 of "Children's Rhymes" where the word "De-Dop" appears. Imagining that "De-Dop" privileges syncopation is to read it as a triumph emblematic of the empowerment gained through signifying. Taking ownership of the realities of hegemony produces an art form that results in the artist turning the notion of a late arrival into a mode for musical (or poetic) delivery. The delayed realization of dreams counters the appropriation of "Be-Bop" into "Re-Bop" as commodification itself receives its redress via the musical concept of syncopation, which turns the concept of delay into a mode of vocal delivery. Equally important, the artistic demands of syncopation deftly resist being appropriated easily through mimicry.

Hence, Hughes's sequence highlights the transformation of hidden violence into art. This violence is nowhere more evident than in the poems "Shame on You" and "World War II." In each poem, the speaker chastises Harlem's black citizens for not remembering the past violence that has led to death. In "Shame on You," the speaker's anger burns through the page as he seethes over the fact that Harlem has no appropriate memorial for John Brown. Furthermore, in the next poem in the sequence, titled "World War II," the speaker further challenges readers to remember that World War II was not a "grand time" (12), but a time in which people died. Hughes thus remembers the forgotten dead in *Montage*, modeling in verse what bop does in song. He transcodes the cultural memory of violence into poetry.

Hughes's art appears to have been deeply influenced by photography. This influence allowed Hughes to activate photography's ability for "making time stand still" and "to make memory possible" (Goldsby 229). Photography does this where film fails. Photos stop and hold viewer's attention to their subjects, while film's constant motion forces spectators to discern all too quickly whether the subject is as interesting as the technology and editing that makes the means of viewing such subjects possible. With *Montage*, Hughes created a photo-text to force viewers to make connections between the past and present.

The inability to detect the potential remainders and traces of American lynching culture in "Dream Deferred" reveals at least two things simultaneously. It reaffirms the powerful role censorship played in advancing Hughes's poetic complexity. It also reminds us of the need to read Hughes's poetry within the cultural context of the 1950s, when the idea of lynching again took on new and broader meanings.

This context also illuminates how "Dream Deferred" functions in *Montage*. In this sequence, "Dream Deferred" may assert that one's dreams can now be added to the list of things that America lynches. As such, the loss of such dreams serves as another way to understand Hughes's assertion that Harlem is "a community in transition" (*CW* 3: 21). Apparently, even as its citizens move forward, they are finding that the literal aspect of lynching has become figurative. It has extended its powers of control through hegemony. *Montage* reveals a community that has renewed its commitment to respond in varying ways even as history proves to be more cyclic than linear.

Given this political and cultural context, would it be surprising that Hughes would use analogy in 1951? Readers have long felt that Hughes's sequence reminds us that art can create a "façade of carefree happiness" (Tracy 230). Here, perhaps, pain is not just concealed, but is also the wellspring from which memorable imagery comes forth. In "Dream Deferred," Hughes posited Harlem as an "unfinished history whose parameters stretch forward and backward in time" (Summers-Brenner 280). Reading the poem through the lens of the photographic analogy suggests the need for a reevaluation of its past and present remainders of lynching. Just when lynching itself was undergoing a change from mob violence to domestic terrorism, Hughes's poetry was forced to change as well.

If we choose to read the poem this way, we see how Hughes negotiated censorship in regard to his mainstream audience. In fact, this concealment actually serves to model one of the major points of the sequence of poems that comprise *Montage*. In asserting that black dissatisfaction is hidden beneath smiling faces, Hughes's poem is itself a masked performance in which the imagery, pain, and history of lynching rest latent. This is yet another of Hughes's "functions of masking" as he emphasizes "the politics of the page" (Summers-Brenner 272). Both the human faces that appear in *Montage* and the poetic series mask the deepest sources of their pain. Perhaps Langston Hughes's "Dream Deferred" was intended to simultaneously mask and reveal some of the pain that had accumulated in the deepest tributaries of Harlem's soul. As such, Hughes's poem is yet another art form (seen here in action) that models, demonstrates, and serves as a particular example of what bebop and other forms of black artistic expression do by concealing one of the root sources leading to and informing its final enunciation. Hughes's sequence reminds us that varying combinations of joy, pain, and delay result in beautiful art.

What happened when the imagery of lynching replaced direct verbal assertions is that no one seemed to notice. Perhaps that was precisely the point. Yet why would Hughes use an analogy so complex that no one would immediately recognize it? Did he have future readers in mind? Can we imagine it as a creative moment embedded in the literary record, waiting to be uncovered by future readers who would be well attuned to the coded language used to describe lynching? Or has it been there all along, with its present recognition serving as a reminder that for decades Hughes has been read through lenses that suppress his complexity, highlight his archetypal speakers, and revel in his musicality? The unveiling of the power of these entrenchments can surprise even devoted scholars, who are often the first to resist and deflect the interpretive force of critical frameworks. In the end, "Dream Deferred" reveals a great deal to us about the habitual nature of our reading habits as well as the structures that brought, hold, and seek to extend Hughes firmly within the canonical tradition.

Such a hermeneutics of suspicion against interpretative frameworks seeks to recover the complexity of Hughes's poetry. With "Dream Deferred," will our lenses yield to the possibility that suggestivity stands in place of statement, that Hughes offered his readers a poem that reads like a series of pictures? Did Hughes speak about the loss of dreams with a powerful elusiveness? If so, we come to ascertain the most important fact of all: through the use of ambiguity, Hughes could only show, his mainstream audience, through highly allusive imagery, what it felt like to wait for a dream to be fulfilled: he dared not tell. This is what it took to pass a poem about lynching in 1951. This may be what Hughes wanted us to see more clearly when he placed "Dream Deferred" immediately after "Not for Publication" in 1966.

Saying was more dangerous than showing. Talking about lynching overtly would have left him open to the type of attacks waged against others such as Paul Robeson. Such topics were not for publication unless they were submerged. As Hughes himself suggested in "Not for Publication," talking about this subject left you feeling crucified.

In the few years following 1953, the national consciousness would be reawakened to the horrors of lynching in its more recognizable forms. Ever adapting, Hughes moved away from using analogy as he instead created poetry that stood as an important counternarrative.

They lynch me still in Mississippi

Langston Hughes, "The Negro"

4

Poetry as Counternarrative

Retelling History

Because the cultural climate surrounding him in the 1950s consisted of blatant censorship and repeated accusations of communism, Hughes's poetry deserves to be read within a framework in which he had to show discretion when speaking about lynching. Hughes discovered strategies to address the topic of lynching in his poetry without being censored. He sometimes passed his poetry by "articulating other voices with such force and clarity that readers have assumed his complete disappearance from the poem" (Ponce 528). How and where Hughes passed poems about lynching is a subject that deserves to be revisited.

It is important to note that, in regard to the notion of passing, I am distinguishing between Hughes's genres and his audience. Simple's dialogic structure and humor inherently distanced the speakers from their author, and Hughes was certainly able to speak indignantly in the black press and in specific places such as the *Chicago Defender*.

In addition, selective audiences could also see Hughes address lynching on the stage before the 1950s. Hughes's 1943 play *For This We Fight* was performed before "a Negro Freedom Rally on June 7, 1943, in Madison Square Garden, New York City," where it "played to a sold-out crowd" (*CW* 6: 437). This play made extensive reference to the long history of lynching in America. In the play, we hear that Nat Turner was "shot hung" (*CW* 6: 444) and the white sympathizer Elijah Lovejoy was dragged off to be "lynched for freedom" as the mob cried out: "Kill him! Lynch him! Kill him" (*CW* 6: 445). As Hughes chronicles the African American struggle for freedom up to the present, a Klansman holds a rope in his hands before declaring "it will be wrapped around you next if you don't make yourself scarce before nightfall" (*CW* 6: 452). By the end of the play, cast members declare their desire for many things, including the "freedom from fear" and for President Roosevelt to speak up "for the anti-lynching bill" (*CW* 6: 460–61).

However, Hughes's poetry was directly linked to his own political thinking well into the late 1950s. Hughes's own testimony before HUAC further reveals this fact. Of the seven literary works about which Hughes was questioned, five were poems; the other two were a play and an essay. During the questioning, Chief Counsel Roy Cohn incorrectly referred to Hughes's play *Scottsboro Limited* as a poem (United States 977). Worse, in trying to refer to one of Hughes's essays, Cohn did not know the genre, the correct title, or the correct place of publication (United States 985). In short, Hughes experienced more liberty in genres that excited less public interest than did poetry.

Representatives of the dominant culture were unwilling to let a man whom they considered to be, at the very least, a communist sympathizer berate America for its lynchings of African Americans. Unable to simply examine their own hypocrisy regarding the nation's professed core principles of freedom and justice, they incorrectly suspected that such critical attacks veiled deeper anti-American political purposes. They feared that his rhetoric was part of a larger underground movement called communism, which appeared to be bent on either undermining the structure of the established U.S. government or overthrowing the country.

Hughes learned that his identity could be coded differently in varying contexts. As we have seen, Hughes knew how to pass for Mexican while traveling by train through Texas. In Russia, he was greeted as a comrade in the 1930s. During his first trip to Africa, he learned that the native people would not regard his skin as dark enough to earn the title black. Hughes learned where and how he would and would not be allowed to pass on a personal level, and his poetry displays this same awareness. His negotiation of this constraint reveals that Hughes could simultaneously veil and document American lynching culture. Hughes's poetic designs that passed despite the constraints of censorship and red baiting reveal that he was unwilling to void this all-too-important subject from his writings. A reevaluation of his poetic works recovers his inventiveness, ambition, and determination in the face of these strict parameters.

This chapter explores Hughes's ability to successfully negotiate censorship so that he could still address the subject of lynching in his poetry. Hughes's references to lynching pass as he discusses the subject under the guise of simply retelling history. Hughes's poem "The Negro" is the central example of this strategy. In addition to retelling history, Hughes's work serves as a counternarrative to published news accounts of lynchings that appeared in the press. Hughes's poems, which appear to be only retelling history, first passed because they were presented in the guise of revisiting past events. They didn't read like rhetorical pleas for social change. Thus, they passed because they appear to concern issues that are distant and resolved rather than temporally close and in need of redress. Hughes's poetic counternarratives stand out because of their surprising complexity. "Mississippi" will be examined in this chapter as one of Hughes's most important achievements in regard to writing counternarratives. In this poem, Hughes braids together allusions and autocitation as he rides new social currents that allow him to continue to extend and explore innovative ways of deepening our understanding of lynching.

Retelling History

Hughes invoked a deceptively simple strategy for passing his poems about American lynching culture on to the general public in the 1950s. This strategy included the "quasi-(in)visible dissent" practiced in the "rewriting" of "specific historical or cultural events" (Roman 4). By appearing to be only retelling past history, his creative works read like narrative accounts focused on recovering cultural memories rather than angry protests pushing for immediate social or legislative change.

It is important to retrace when Hughes started this strategy of retelling history. He began applying the practice of retelling history around the same time he was drafting ideas for *Montage* in the late 1940s. In fact, he first passed several of his lynching poems into his collection

One-Way Ticket (1949); yet the high point of this practice came ten years later with "The Negro." Thinking back to an earlier image of Hughes testifying before HUAC in 1953 reminds us of a startling irony. Had the committee decided to look in the very books placed on the table before Hughes, they would not have had to look far for a critique of American racism. Several of Hughes's poems that portrayed lynching under the guise of retelling history sat right before them under the cover of *One-Way Ticket*. The title poem of the collection that had been published only four years before this interrogation makes it clear why the speaker leaves the South by train and heads for the North. Near the end of the third stanza of the poem, he states he is tired of lynch mobs. Hughes also offered his readers four "Silhouettes" of lynching in this collection. In "Blue Bayou," he continues the association between sunsets and lynching culture that first appeared in "The Negro Speaks of Rivers"; furthermore, the poem continues the dialogic and multivoiced narrative structure of "Christ in Alabama" as the mob, oppressed black lynch victim, and speaker in the poem each take turns speaking. "Silhouette," the third poem in the cycle, reads the lynched victim's body as a sign to the world of how white women are protected from black rapists. Hughes's poetry serves as the immortal site for which youth will never wither away as "Lynching Song" suggests that the lynched body refuses to die.

Perhaps the clearest way to read this refusal of death mentioned in "Lynching Song" is by placing it in context with the stage directions Hughes wrote for his play *Don't You Want to Be Free?* which premiered in 1938. The play ran for over two seasons, and Hughes himself declared that it was "probably the most performed Negro play of our time, having had 135 performances in Harlem when it was done in 1937–38, and some 200 more in various cities and at most of the Negro colleges throughout the country, Wilberforce, Howard, Talledega [*sic*], Dillard, Atlanta University, etc." (*CW* 5: 538). Hughes was very specific in his stage directions for the play: "no curtains or stage effects other than the lynch rope which hangs at the back, center, throughout the entire performance, and serves as a symbol of Negro oppression" (*CW* 5: 570). Hughes even interprets the play as he comments about how the noose is to be used. He designates that the character known simply as YOUNG MAN place it around his neck during one of the scenes and then take "his head from the noose on the words, 'Not I.' Symbolic of the eternal resurrection of hope of an oppressed people" (*CW* 5: 570). This interpretive directive from Hughes helps us read the authorial intention behind this poem. The words "Not I" that appear in the play are also the last words of the poem "Lynching Song." Hughes braided his poetry together with his work in other genres as he retold the history of oppression from an African American perspective.

Hughes passed his most significant reference to contemporary lynching in a poem titled "The Negro." His strategy worked because he spent eighteen of the poem's nineteen lines referencing a history that happened in the distant past, and only one short line commenting on the subject of lynching. This short commentary is similar to his approach in "The Negro Speaks of Rivers."

In fact, Hughes first published a poem he titled "The Negro" in *Crisis* in January 1922. Later that year, in March, it was published in its same format in *Current Opinion*. Hughes retitled the work "Proem" for its later appearance in his first poetry collection, *The Weary Blues* (1926), then altered the title back to "The Negro" for its appearance in *The Dream Keeper* (1932). In all of the above instances, only the name of the poem was altered: the sixteenth line of the poem remained the same in every case. Hughes wrote: "I've been a victim: / The Belgians cut off my hands in the Congo. / They lynch me now in Texas" (14–16). As we have seen in the earlier discussion of "The Negro Speaks of Rivers," Hughes associated the state of Texas with American lynching culture from the beginning of his lifetime through the 1920s. His tour of the South and his response to the Scottsboro case resulted in his topophobic association extending even farther to such areas as Alabama. Hughes's choice to publish and republish this poem on four different occasions in 1922, 1926, 1932, and 1959 suggests that he thought enough of its content to keep its ideas in the forefront of readers' consciousnesses. Even more importantly, Hughes set this important poem off from all others in his first full collection of poems, *The Weary Blues*. The poem appeared alone as the introductory poem to this collection, serving as an overview of the themes that would continue to appear throughout his poetic career.

The main idea and central thematic thrust center on a comparison of violent oppression throughout history and across the political boundaries of the world. Is Hughes suggesting in this poem that the harm of having one's hand cut off in the Congo is surprisingly less severe than being lynched in America? Both are clearly horrific forms of terrorism, and Hughes's poem forces readers to compare the two.

Moreover, his word choice of "now" contrasts sharply with his historical reference to what happened in the Congo in the past.[1] The time of King Leopold's reign, 1885–1908, when such events happened in the Congo, has passed; lynching in Texas is happening now, in the present. Such a reading seems ultimately to have its most important resonance in reminding readers that American lynching culture is not just equal to Belgian oppression; rather, it is far worse. We find out more about the oppressors than the oppressed in this poem. The fact that American oppressors exceed that of the Belgians in regard to historical immediacy as well as the degree of violence serves as a shocking and terrifying unsettling of the dominant culture's widely accepted historical narrative of America.

The *Selected Poems* edition of Hughes's poetry that appeared in 1959 included a significant revision to this poem. Hughes seems to have anticipated that the more extensive space allotted in the poem to historical background would allow it to pass in the climate of the 1950s. Hughes shortened the title of his poem to "Negro"; more importantly, for the first time in its publication history, Hughes altered line 16 to read: "They lynch me still in Mississippi."

This revision suggests at least two things about Hughes's poetry during the historical context of 1959. First, Hughes was not going to drop the subject of lynching from his work entirely. Instead, he was intent on making it more visible than most writers would dare. Despite all the variables that created the cultural climate of high nationalism in the United States at this time, Hughes would uncover a means for negotiating it. Here, he stands against the pressures of red-baiting, HUAC, and fears among publishers by quickly reminding everyone that lynching is still continuing in America. The only difference is that it has seemingly shifted in intensity from one center (Texas) to another (Mississippi). Only the places have changed. At first gloss it appears that Hughes may have offered this place revision given the very public 1955 lynching of Emmett Till in Mississippi.

This shifting locale is significant to understanding patterns in Hughes's development in speaking out against such violence. Equally important is his important reminder of time. "Still" further elevates American violence over what came to fruition in the Congo. King Leopold's reign of terror spanned approximately twenty-five years (1885–1908). Hughes is reminding us that American violence is not only more intense, but it also casts its shadow over citizens for a far longer period. Hughes's revision forces us to recount his previous thirty-seven years of campaigning against American lynching culture (1922–59).

Furthermore, his resentment is measurable as he portrays the eras of Rome, colonial America, and the Congo as mere precursors to the oppressions experienced in contemporary Mississippi. The present moment captured in the earliest word "now" and reiterated in the revised "still" is so easy to overlook that it gets ignored by many readers. Again, it is similar to what happens in approaches to "The Negro Speaks of Rivers." Both poems have earned a reputation for having captured the history of black citizens at the expense of examining their contemporary contexts. Just as the Nile River and the pyramids overshadow Hughes's own passage across the Mississippi River in "The Negro Speaks of Rivers," here the presence of Africa and the Congo work to veil the culminating statement of continued oppression and violence in America.

In regard to Hughes himself, we might imagine him venting his anger against the constraints of censorship, which have relegated his statements against lynching to the space of a mere single-line revision of one of his poems. In revisiting this deft revision, we feel the force and inertia this diminutive statement unleashes on 1950s American lynching culture. Moreover, the earlier publication date of 1922 creates the illusion that Hughes has merely included one of his older poems in his *Selected Poems*. This makes his revision nearly impossible to locate as a comment on a contemporary social horror. Hence, it passed.

This poem not only passed republication in *Selected Poems*, but Hughes also read it out loud in Washington, D.C., in October 1962. After being greeted at the White House by Mrs. Kennedy, Hughes joined almost three dozen other poets for the first national poetry festival. Hughes placed special emphasis on the original publication date of this poem during his formal poetry reading, as he quipped that the poem was the opening poem of his first ever book (Rampersad 2: 357). Again, he was suggesting to his listeners that it was an old poem that offered no new critique of American racial violence. However, this single–line revision took on added significance as his opening poem at the festival was "Still Here," a poem in which Hughes's speaker announces that despite the fact that he's been "scared and battered" (1), he remains defiantly "still here!" (8).

The poem's ability to pass as a retelling of history reveals a great deal about its readers. Of most concern is the possibility that a reader in the late 1950s would perhaps acknowledge such lynchings as inevitable social practice; worse, twenty-first-century readers are sometimes so completely unaware of the practice of lynching that they simply ignore the line all together. At all levels, many of our educational institutions have made contemporary readers more knowledgeable about George Washington and Julius Caesar than they have about the lynchings of Jesse Washington and Emmett Till.

►•◄

Selected Poems contains three other poems that address lynching under the guise of documenting old history. "Blue Bayou," "Silhouette," and "Song for a Dark Girl" appear in the collection. Given the progression of this sequence in the collection, these three poems make their way into the collection as if they describe a past reality. They are located as motivations for leaving the South. This movement is completed by the three poems that follow them. In "The South," the speaker concludes that he will now go north, and the next poem, "Bound No'th Blues," documents his journey. "One-Way Ticket" continues this movement. Like many of Hughes's other works, this poem "promotes displacement" as an empowering experience (Soto 171).

These poems make it appear that such atrocities are a thing of the past that motivated blacks to engage in the in-migration to northern locals such as Chicago and Harlem. In short, it is only the single-line revision in "Negro" that reminds readers that lynching is a contemporary issue in need of social redress. It is not likely that Hughes suddenly felt lynching had gone away and was now a thing of the past. If he had, he would not have taken the time to revise the line in "Negro" or ensure that this poem was part of his high-profile program in Washington, D.C. It was not so much a necessary updating of an outdated poem as it was his choice to find an opening through which his disdain for lynching could be expressed.

Selected Poems and *The Langston Hughes Reader*

Extending Hughes's own use of analogy as discussed in the previous chapter, why might we consider reading *The Langston Hughes Reader* (1958) and *The Selected Poems of Langston Hughes* (1959) as lynched texts? Given the cultural climate in which they were published, neither includes any of Hughes's long attacks against American lynching culture. Among others, "Christ in Alabama," "Mississippi," "Three Lynching

Songs," and "The Bitter River" are nowhere to be found in either collection. Given the immediacy of what is perhaps the most documented lynching in American history only three years earlier, the lynching of Emmett Till, this absence is more likely explained by the repercussions Hughes had to avoid among publishers and readers rather than a choice to drop this issue from his campaign.

Even more interesting, Hughes's "Not for Publication" appeared in print in the international publication *Black Orpheus* in 1959 rather than in his *Selected Poems* or *The Langston Hughes Reader*. Published by the Ministry of Education in Ibadan, Nigeria, editors Ulli Beier and Janheinz Jahn called *Black Orpheus* "A Journal of African and Afro-American Literature." Hughes's interest in Africa dated back at least to his first trip there in 1923. This interest had been growing even more recently as he had read his poetry to the accompaniment of a Nigerian drummer in celebration of African Freedom Day at Carnegie Hall on April 15, 1959 (Rampersad 2: 299). One month later, "Not for Publication" appeared in the pages of *Black Orpheus*, where his five poems were prominently listed in the magazine's table of contents. It was an important change from Hughes's inclusion of the poem in *Crisis*.

Racism in America is again juxtaposed with "Africa" just as it was in the 1953 edition of *Crisis*; however, three other poems were also included. These poems display a tone of frustration rare in Hughes's work. "So" (retitled "Impasse" when it appeared later in *The Panther and the Lash*) features perhaps the only time Hughes ever used profanity in print. Appearing directly after "Not for Publication," "So" extends the preceding poem's idea of "talking" as the speaker states that he could say who he is, but that the imagined listener probably doesn't "Give a damn" (8). Hughes's poetic sequence ends with the speaker linking the plight of black Americans and Africans by suggesting, in "African Question Mark," that each must fight together against fear and other men.

By placing "Not for Publication" in the international *Black Orpheus*, Hughes deliberately declined the more obvious opportunity to publish it in his *Selected Poems* (1959) or *The Langston Hughes Reader* (1958). *Selected Poems* had appeared in print on March 23, 1959, a mere two months before the publication of his works in *Black Orpheus*. Rather than include this volatile poem in *Selected Poems*, Hughes instead included seven never-before-published works.[2] More telling still, Hughes had spaces to fill in his *Selected Poems*. A handwritten note located on a draft of the poem "Tambourines" makes this clear: "Drafts of a poem written especially to fill an empty page in the final proofs of my *Selected Poems*."[3] By drafting an apolitical poem like "Tambourines" to replace the more ambitious "Not for Publication" in *Selected Poems*, Hughes avoided further crucifixion. Hughes also wrote another new poem for *The Langston Hughes Reader* a year earlier. "Pastoral" recounts blooming flowers as reminders of Jesus' return. "Pastoral" offers a very different fate for Christ as imagined in "Not for Publication." Hughes displayed anger and frustration when the opportunity presented itself in an international publication. This stands in sharp contrast to the docility that permeates poems such as "Tambourines" and "Pastoral."

Hughes himself appears to have had ambivalent feelings about his *Selected Poems*. On the one hand, he is very excited to use the appearance of the book in print to help him earn a coveted nomination for the NAACP's most prestigious award, the Spingarn Award. After having already written a letter to Arna Bontemps listing in detail his accomplishments, Hughes more than nudges Bontemps to use the appearance of this collection of poems as another of his merits: "I send you under separate cover Knopf's Spring Catalogue marketing my *Selected Poems* so you might send it onto the Spingarn Award Selection Committee if you deem it now the moment to make that nomination" (Bontemps and Hughes 378). No doubt its appearance contributed to Hughes winning this award the next year as he followed in the footsteps of recent recipients Jackie Robinson, Duke Ellington, and Martin Luther King Jr.

More revealing still is a comment Hughes made in 1960 (a year after the release of *Selected Poems*). While revising his anthology of *New Negro Poets*, Indiana University Press demanded that Hughes eliminate controversial poems about racial ideas. Hughes responded to poet Margaret Danner: "Loud and angry race cries such as you and I are accustomed to give are not at the moment 'comme il faut; or à la mode' as poetic style. (But don't worry, I expect they will be again in due time!)" (Rampersad 2: 323).

It is clear that Hughes's *Selected Poems* had a specific audience in mind. In addition to having to avoid overt politics, the collection sought to capitalize on the concurrent interest in linking jazz and poetry. In light of Carl Sandburg's October 1958 appearance on the *Milton Berle Show*, where his poetry was read to the accompaniment of jazz, Bontemps suggested to Hughes that "this would be a terrific way to boom your *Selected Poems*" (Bontemps and Hughes 376–77). Clearly the renewed interest in the connections between jazz and poetry influenced the poetry selections included in the collection.

However, as time distanced Hughes from this collection, his dismay over the process of selection grew. Hughes hints at the lack of real ownership he had in selecting the poems when he writes to Bontemps in early 1961. He states that "My *Selected Poems* (of a sort, just came out in Italy)" (Bontemps and Hughes 408). His "of a sort" gestures toward the realities of the contextual constraints framing the volume. Nonetheless, Hughes also supplies the specific information about this Italian version in this same letter so that it might be included in one of Italy's United States Information Agency libraries.

The Langston Hughes Reader (1958) offers its readers even less of a clear representation of Hughes's lifelong commitment to writing about lynching than his *Selected Poems* does. Although Hughes included four short stories from his 1934 collection *The Ways of White Folks*, none of the three stories featuring lynching as a central issue are included. "Home," "Father and Son," and "Mother and Child" are nowhere to be found. Whereas Christopher De Santis could justifiably argue that Hughes's short stories reveal his "acute interest in the question of social justice" (*CW* 15: 2), no common citizen, student, or scholar reading *The Langston Hughes Reader* would report such a discovery.

This pattern continued with the selections included from *Laughing to Keep from Crying* (1952). Published in the year prior to his testimony before HUAC, Hughes referenced sarcastically in "One Friday Morning" that the "negro in America is . . . sometimes lynched" (*CW* 15: 217). "Little Old Spy" captures Hughes being followed by a spy while in Havana. As expected, neither of these stories is included in *The Langston Hughes Reader*. In fact, poetry itself seems censored, as if other genres in and of themselves are far safer ventures. Aside from the complete *Montage of a Dream Deferred*, only eleven of Hughes's poems are included. This is a stunning number considering that Hughes considered himself first and foremost a poet. Moreover, the volume is more than five hundred pages long. Was there more than a marketing strategy at work in omitting poetry from this collection?

It is important to note briefly one work that did make its way into *The Langston Hughes Reader*. The Simple story "There Ought to Be a Law" is included in this collection. The story illustrates how Hughes negotiated this time period effectively in prose. After asserting in typical fashion with equal parts of sagacity and comic humor that there ought to be a law establishing "Game Preserves for Negroes," Simple states that "Congress ought to set aside some place where we can go and nobody can jump on us and beat us, neither lynch us. . . . Colored folks rate as much protection as a buffalo, or a deer" (*CW* 7: 96).

This attack on American lynching culture informs how Hughes was still able to address this subject in this collection. This prose commentary passed because it was countered by the seemingly more intelligent Boyd, who earlier asserted that "there are a lot of good white people in this world" (61). As others have said in general, Boyd's statement in this particular instance seemingly counters and cancels the superior logic and argumentation of Simple's historical and poignant rhetoric. This dialogic exchange allows Boyd to appear to be wiser. But Boyd is really learning from Simple rather than teaching him, and the rhetorical nuance of dialogism coupled with unquestionable humor allows Hughes to pass such a prose piece into *The Langston Hughes Reader*. Simple originally spoke with Hughes himself in these columns before Hughes invented Boyd (Harper 78). The invention of Boyd clearly helped to distance the poet from these fictional discussions. We might conclude that laughing masks the crying, and the dialogic nature of two seemingly opposing viewpoints works in the genre of prose to cancel the ability to fully connect Hughes's personal political stance with either character.

Perhaps it is no coincidence that Hughes turned to writing his Simple columns even more during these years. For a general audience, poems would always contain a voice that would be assumed to be that of Hughes. Such an audience was less likely to recognize the existence of a speaker other than Hughes himself in these poems. However, in the dialogic conversations between Simple and his friend, Hughes's own voice and ears gradually gave way to the guise of Boyd. By making it difficult to pin down exactly where Hughes's opinions resided in these conversations, the dialogic interplay served as protection from attacks. Perhaps it is the dialogic nature and the parody of these conversations that allows them to enlighten readers without being censored. Even attentive readers of *The Langston Hughes Reader* and *Selected Poems* would be unlikely to discern in those works Hughes's sustained lifelong campaign against U.S. lynching culture. In fact, the textual evidence of such a campaign would seem to have been almost entirely lacking.

These collections greatly altered the reception and perception of Hughes's poetry for readers, teachers, and scholars for as long as the next thirty-five years. *The Langston Hughes Reader* was republished in

1971 without any changes from its 1958 format. More importantly, it would not be until 1994 that Hughes's poetry would be restored with the appearance of *The Collected Poems of Langston Hughes*. This date is thirty-five years after *Selected Poems*, a work that is still readily available even today, having last been republished in 1990. Furthermore, it was not until 2001 that Hughes's entire oeuvre received the critical attention it deserved with the seventeen-volume collected works published by the University of Missouri Press. Between 1959 and 1994, readers seeking a comprehensive overview of Hughes's poetry turned to *Selected Poems*. Although his more volatile works had appeared elsewhere in print, his *Selected Poems* served as a de facto version of his collected poems. Hughes's critical responses to lynching in this volume were noticeable by their absence.

Fight for Freedom

Hughes continued his strategy of retelling history well into the early 1960s. Hughes invoked this strategy to address the subject of lynching as he wrote the definitive history of the NAACP. *Fight for Freedom: The Story of the NAACP* appeared in 1962. Although it purports to be a history of the efforts of the NAACP, Hughes's narrative reads much more like a history of lynching in twentieth-century America. In fact, the subject of lynching is addressed continuously throughout the text. It is impossible to ignore what Christopher De Santis has wisely noted as "Hughes's unconstrained disgust for the many incidents of racial violence, prejudice and discrimination that motivate the NAACP to act. Hughes gives particular emphasis to the NAACP's long-term campaign against lynching, often describing in horrific detail the crimes committed to terrorize African Americans into submission" (*CW* 10: 15).

An analysis of Hughes's references to lynching captures just how well he knew this subject. Hughes establishes that lynching was the primary subject that led to the formation of the NAACP. He cites Mary White Ovington's 1906 visit to Alabama as a moment where she learned that black men "might be lynched without anyone ever being punished for the crime" (*CW* 10: 39). This trip as well as a 1908 incident in Springfield, Illinois, in which a mob "lynched a Negro barber and an 84-year-old man for no reason at all" motivates Miss Ovington to seek "to remedy the deplorable state of race relations"(*CW* 10: 39). By 1910, a formal conference took place in New York, and soon thereafter the NAACP was born.

Hughes also reminds readers that, in one of the first cases ever handled by the NAACP, the organization called for the "arrest and conviction of the lynchers" responsible for the "mob burning of a Negro laborer in Coatesville, Pennsylvania" (*CW* 10: 44).

Hughes's knowledge of lynching is specific. He recounts the exact number of lynch victims in the United States for 1901 and offers this account for later years: "In that year [1913] 79 persons were lynched. In 1912 the count was 63—an average of more than one mass murder a week. An expanded NAACP was a necessity" (*CW* 10: 45). Hughes clearly sees the NAACP's role as one that is meant to offset the increase of spectacle lynching. It is also likely that Hughes recounted such figures from memory. In the autobiography *I Wonder as I Wander*, published in 1956, Hughes recounted: "In that year, 1931, there had been twelve lynchings in the South. Several of my poems were about voting and lynching; and I always read some of them on each program, as well as one or two poems about the Scottsboro Case" (*CW* 14: 81).

Hughes also devotes five consecutive pages, under the titles "Cause for a Holiday" and "The Shame of America," to addressing lynching in *Fight for Freedom*. Hughes quotes an eight-page article of the NAACP's *Crisis* that informed readers around the country about the practice of souveniring. Hughes had likely first read the article before he ever took his first trip through Texas. Readers learn that following the lynching of Jesse Washington, his teeth were sold for "$5 apiece and the chain that bound him $0.25 a link" (*CW* 10: 51). He also recounts the history of the Dyer antilynching bill, exact lynching statistics for the years 1916 and 1917, financial contributions by Philip Peabody and Moorfield Storey on behalf of the organization's antilynching fund, and the NAACP's 1919 study *Thirty Years of Lynching in the United States*.

In regard to this text, Hughes does not miss the opportunity to document the sadistic practice of lynching. He recounts no fewer than seven of the most horrific accounts of lynchings chronicled in *Thirty Years of Lynching*, including the subsequent death of a lynched woman's unborn child and the "15,000 men, women and children" who cheered after the burning of Ell Person, believing him to still be alive after his death because "they saw the charred remains move as does meat on a hot frying pan" (*CW* 10: 53). As with his poetry, Hughes held nothing back when it came to addressing such events. Moreover, as suggested earlier regarding "Dream Deferred," the connection between food and lynching was used by both African American writers and the dominant culture.

Hughes references this subject so often in this text that he even attempts to avoid the redundancy of the word "lynching." Hughes creates variety by instead referring to it as "torture-death" (*CW* 10: 73). Searching for other descriptions, he also says that victims were "done to death by mobs in mass orgies of violence" (*CW* 10: 39).

Eventually, Hughes covers the antilynching efforts of Walter White and the lynchings of Cordie Cheek, Mack Parker, and Felton Turner. Because lynching culture intimidated even where the silhouette of a swaying body was not present, Hughes also carefully documents a threat received by Thurgood Marshall in Mississippi, who was told "he had better get out of town before sunset" (*CW* 10: 150). This text reminds us that Hughes invoked the strategy of retelling history even into the early 1960s in a genre other than poetry. Writing a history about the NAACP obviously provided a perfect opportunity.

Counternarrative

Often the artist, not the fact-finding journalist, offers the reader the emotional background missing from many newsprint accounts of lynchings. In fact, the historical recovery of the way lynchings were covered by the press suggests that "lynching was one of those experiences reporters were not allowed to represent fully, naturally it fell to writers of fiction, not journalists, to do it justice. . . . [L]ynching can be understood as one of those pressing topics that literature took up when journalism fell short" (Lutes 457). Many mainstream newspaper accounts of lynchings reported only factual evidence. The *Atlanta Constitution* reported a 1935 lynching in a purely unemotional tone:

> Abe Young, a negro, was hanged to an oak tree in a schoolyard three miles east of here this afternoon by a mob of about 50 white men. . . .
>
> He was placed atop a small coach automobile, with a rope around his neck. The other end of the rope was suspended to a tree. The car was driven out from under him and he was left dangling at the end of the rope. (Ginzburg 225)

Focusing on the act of lynching rather than the details that led to the murder ignores the emotional tenor of such encounters, which Hughes's literature provides.

Many reports of lynching were also so brief that literature itself found a way to expand their narratives and set them within a larger context. Take, for example, another representative newspaper article from 1934 included in its entirety: "Accused of writing an 'indecent and insulting' letter to a young Hinds County white girl, James Sanders, 25-year-old negro, was riddled with bullets late today by a mob of armed citizens" (Ginzburg 220). This narrative is most notable for its absences. Readers would have no way of interpreting the legitimacy of the accusation, the fervor of the mob, or the contents of the letter.

Worse, many newspaper accounts subverted "the impact of white aggression" (Smith McKoy 48). Here the press turned murderers into victims:

> A bent, little old man today stood on the porch of his simple farm home and said a mob "done me wrong" because it killed the Negro accused of attacking and killing his twenty-three-year-old daughter after assuring the old man that he would "have the first shot." . . .
>
> "They done me wrong about the killing," said the aged father as he wept. "They promised me they would bring him up to my house before they killed him and let me have the first shot. That's what I wanted." (Ginzburg 224)

Here the lynch victim is so markedly erased by the man who missed his opportunity in the extralegal execution that the entire lynching narrative is reversed. The lynch victim does not even count. The mob gets blamed for not following its procedures of decorum and for enacting the father's vengeance rather than for the horror of this particular murder. It is instead the father who has been injured, and the real victim, who, in this case, was the viciously mutilated Claude Neal, is simply an irrelevant object of amusement. The mob is chastised for not honoring its promises rather than for what actually happened to Neal, who was dismembered and then forced to swallow his own genitals.

Of course, not all the press coverage of lynchings maintained such a distanced stance from the actual victims. New York's *Amsterdam News* sought to give a greater voice to lynching victims. Its account of the lynching of the sixty-six-year-old Rev. Isaac Simmons in New Orleans in 1944 included the complete eyewitness account given by the victim's son Eldridge Simmons.[4] But even these published accounts lacked the full narrative power available to literature. Hughes's literary responses to lynching serve as a much-needed corrective to mainstream sources, and what they offer extends beyond the less available and sympathetic narratives of such papers as *Amsterdam News*.

"Father and Son," *Mulatto, The Barrier,* and "Georgia Dusk"

It is important to take a retrospective glance back at Hughes's ability to offer counternarratives before considering the culmination of this poetic achievement that occurs in the poem "Mississippi." In constructing counternarratives in varying works, Hughes often borrowed ideas from one genre to recontextualize them in another. For example, ideas that first appeared in his play *Mulatto* reappeared later in the short story "Father and Son" only to reemerge again in the form of the opera *The Barrier*. In fact, as R. Baxter Miller has asserted, "no single genre ever imprisoned Langston Hughes, who rebelled against formal limits as easily as he opposed social ones" (119). This approach also applied specifically to his work on the subject of lynching, which braids its way through Hughes's oeuvre to span genres such as his plays, short stories, operas, and poetry.

Hughes's first ever play is filled with references to American lynching culture that serve as a counternarrative to the information published by news sources. Apparently written during the summer of 1930, *Mulatto* was first staged on Broadway in 1935, where it ran for more than a year before it "toured for two seasons" (*CW* 5: 17–18). For the next twenty-four years, it was the "longest-running Broadway production by a black writer until Lorraine Hansberry's *A Raisin in the Sun* in 1959" (*CW* 15: 5). Hughes's portrayal draws attention to white male sexual desire as the root problem in rural Georgia's race relations. As a result, the mulatto Robert is confused about his identity as the son of his black mother, Cora, and the white Colonel Tom. Wanting the privileges afforded other white citizens but receiving the same treatment as blacks, Robert kills Colonel Tom in a rage intended to eradicate the most evil element in the equation. The fact that Robert strangles his father with his bare hands seems to be a symbolic turn on the practice where white men usually hang blacks. Robert spends the rest of the play running from the lynch mob.

After escaping at sunset, he attempts to elude the lynch mob's dogs by running through the swamp in the hope of not being tracked, caught, hung, and burned. Such pursuit suggests that the reference to dogs in Hughes's poem "Gal's Cry for a Dying Lover" (1927) is the poetic plea of a woman who fears her man is on the verge of being caught and lynched. It is perhaps the idea of such howling dogs as a memory intensifier that helps us read Hughes's poem "Suburban Evening" (1967) within the context of lynching. Readers of this poem wonder if the speaker becomes afraid after hearing sounds that might remind them of a past memory of bloodhounds hot on the trail of a potential victim.

Before being caught, Robert shoots himself. This decision reminds us that although Georgia led the nation in documented lynchings in 1930, that number does not reflect others who chose suicide. In regard to better understanding these actions, not even statistics offer a comprehensive means for measuring the effects of American lynching culture. For example, newspapers reported that the death of R. J. Tyrone on March 25, 1935, in Hattiesburg, Mississippi, had been ruled a "suicide" by the local coroner despite the fact that Tyrone was found "shot to pieces" after being confronted by an angry white mob (Ginzburg 227). Moreover, the shooting in this play complicates the reading of Hughes's many poems about suicides. Suggesting the possibility that suicide was rarely counted in lynching totals, this play counters the depth and variety of deaths that the press may not label as a lynching.

Despite the fact that Robert clearly murders his father, Hughes considered this play to represent the behaviors of this community's white citizens as much as the frustrations faced by men like Robert. Hughes himself stated in 1961 that "*Mulatto* might be left timeless, since they still behave like that in the backwoods of Georgia. In the big towns, of course, individual sit-ins like Bert's have grown to mass-sit-ins. Otherwise, no difference" (*CW* 5: 17). Hughes reduces Robert's murder to a symbolic form of protest meant to cast light on the sexual passions of white men who consistently use black women as an outlet for their desire. Worse, several references in the play make it clear that Colonel Tom is in fact one of the least abusive white men in the community in this regard.

This Georgia society is one that uses lynching as a means to intimidate black citizens. One white citizen boasts that the community has not had any problems with its black citizens since the lynching that took place there three years earlier. While the lynch mob pursues Robert, Cora is informed of the likelihood that her son will be shot, hung, burned, or all three.

Hughes's short story "Father and Son" follows the same plot as *Mulatto*. Hughes's indictment of white heterosexual males is just as explicit

here as it is in *Mulatto*. In the short story, Bert (instead of Robert) de-
clares his desire to use the gun that is intended for him to kill as many
other white men as possible. However, the ending of the story offers a
significant amendment to that of *Mulatto*: although Robert shoots himself, the mob lynches him anyway. Hughes dislocates the notion of the
suicide by suppressing it from unknowing town residents and the general public by inserting a fictional news clipping at the end of the story.
This newspaper account allows the realms of literature and journalism
to merge. It also inverts the story's focus on white male sexual desire
by juxtaposing it with the compulsive need to lynch. Unable to enjoy
the satisfaction and lust of lynching the living Robert, this fictive newspaper article states that the mob tracked down Robert's brother Willie
Lewis and lynched him, too. There are many historical analogues for this
kind of behavior.[5]

In short, the late edition of that day's newspaper offers false information. It not only suppresses Bert's suicide, but it also implies that
Willie Lewis was involved. Hughes's story undermines the legitimacy of
mainstream newspaper accounts. Hughes's fictional story is more real
than the news itself. Hughes subverts newsprint sources by using their
own text against them. Here the disjunction between Hughes's literary account and that of the press reminds us that Hughes was invested
in portraying such events with greater accuracy and emotional depth
than journalism portrayed to distanced and naïve consumers of print
sources.

"Father and Son" is not the only story that serves as a counternarrative in Hughes's 1934 collection *The Ways of White Folks*. Cora is also
the name of a black woman who appears in the opening story of the
sequence entitled "Cora Unashamed." We learn in very similar fashion
that this slave has only ever been loved by white men. In "Red-Headed
Baby," Hughes offers a further example of miscegenation as the white
Clarence comes back in hopes of loving the black Betsy only to leave
after discovering that his last visit resulted in the birth of his own deaf
baby.

When the roles are reversed in another short story in this collection,
"Mother and Child," the black Douglass faces greater obstacles than em-
barrassment. He has been seeing a married white woman, and members
of the black community discuss the fact that he would have already been
lynched if they were in Mississippi rather than Ohio. By the end of the
story, the man's fate is left unresolved as two women observe that they

are surprised that he has not been lynched, even in Ohio. They speak of being filled with great fear as the story ends without resolution.

More telling still is the story "Home," in which Hughes chronicles the return of the black violinist Roy Williams to his hometown of Hopkinsville, Missouri. After speaking politely with the white Miss Reece on a public sidewalk, Roy is dragged, stripped naked, and left lynched from a tree in the nearby woods. The lynching helps preserve the category of whiteness as she becomes more of an example of white womanhood after this act as opposed to the "old maid" category she occupies earlier in the story (Banks 462). Here again, Hughes's typography collapses the distance between fact and story. Hughes quickly escalates the intensity of the exaggerated accusation against Roy in one sentence as "talking" becomes "insulting," then "attacking, and finally "RAPING" (*CW* 15: 45). Were these allegations reprinted in a newspaper, raping would have been the false accusation that passed for fact. The Romantic tendency to associate inspiration with the Aeolian harp is resignified by Hughes in the final line as Roy's body swings "like a violin for the wind to play" (*CW* 15: 45). The residents of Hopkinsville don't revere imagination—they lynch it. Again, none of these short stories appeared in *The Langston Hughes Reader* in 1958.

Returning to a discussion of how Hughes continued to undermine newspaper reports brings us to his play *Don't You Want to Be Free?* (1943). In this play, Hughes couples staged performance with his poetic texts. In fact, even the stage directions suggest as much as Hughes attempts to signal directors as to the importance of blurring the realms of theater with newsprint sources. Hughes specifies that the lynching in the play include a lighting technique that focuses only "on the face of the dead boy while the NEWSBOYS shout their papers" (*CW* 5: 573). The action described in the play suggests that Hughes is again countering the false reports about lynchings that appear regularly in newspapers. In the play, a black man named Wilbur is lynched over an argument about how much money he is owed. After being hit in the mouth by the overseer Mr. Mallory, Wilbur knocks him unconscious. After receiving advice to run to the swamp to avoid being tracked by dogs, Wilbur is lynched. Immediately thereafter, numerous newsboys enter the stage selling papers about the lynching that are filled with the false information that the lynching was a response to Wilbur being "accused of rape" (*CW* 5: 549). Just as he had done earlier in the short story "Father and Son," Hughes draws our attention to the discrepancies between truth and newsprint.

In addition to countering the narratives sold for mass consumption by the press, *Don't You Want to Be Free?* also places three other important poems within a lynching context. Hughes opens the play by having one of his characters recite the entire poem "Negro." This marks at least the fifth different appearance of this important poem. Immediately following the lynching scene, one of the female characters recites Hughes's "Song for a Dark Girl" (1927). While each of these poems carries overt connections to lynching, "Dream Variations" (1924) stands as a hopeful corrective to the topophobia often associated with being out alone after sunset. It, too, is included in this play as Hughes places the dream of dancing and whirling freely in nature within the context of an idealized African past where there was no threat of being lynched. As such, the speaker dreams of resting in the evening shade under a tree that shows no indication of serving as a site for an execution. In this context, "Dream Variations" is a sort of corrective to American lynching culture: just as "The Negro Speaks of Rivers" reclaimed intimacy with American riverscapes, "Dream Variations" serves as a hopeful reminder of how African Americans can again connect with the natural world once they become free of fear. Distanced from this context, "Dream Variations" would not appear to have the direct relationship to lynching as emphasized in this play.

With *The Barrier* (1950), Hughes took the same basic plot structure from *Mulatto* and "Father and Son" and added the element of music to help shape his opera. Perhaps Hughes took the title from a line in his own short story in which he wrote that "there had been a barrier of fear" between Bert and his father (*CW* 15: 136). This opera was met with "critical hostility, generated more by its story than by its musical or literary merits" (Sanders 67). It passed into production because it is set in 1920s Georgia, which makes it appear to be a story that retells the past. However, its performance was neither accepted nor sustained. Dominant culture in 1950 was not interested in such counternarratives.

The interrelationship between this opera and Hughes's poetry is again important to note. In the prologue to the opera, Hughes begins with twelve lines of verse that later became the poem "Georgia Dusk" (1955). The lines' appearance in the opera predates their first appearance in poetic form by five years. This appearance has been overlooked. By the time it appeared in *The Panther and the Lash*, the poem had undergone some minor revisions from its first form. Revisiting these minor revisions is revealing. Hughes plays off the notion of veiling in the poem. Reading all the intertextual appearances of this plotline, white male obsession with black women, Bert's suicide, and the newspaper's false representation of Willie's involvement are among a myriad of things concealed. In line 6 of the 1950 version of *The Barrier*, Hughes links the concepts of "blood" and "sun" together. His use of the word "dusk" on five different occasions highlights all the dramatic action that takes place in the final scene at sunset.

Finally, linking Georgia's red dirt with the notion of blood is a dramatically imaginative and radical reading of what has contributed to this southern state's unusually red dirt. Rather than a high concentration of iron or clay, Hughes seems to imply that all the blood dripping off of Georgia's lynched bodies has stained it red. At the very least, each new viewing of this ground should be a reminder of the violence and bloodshed that occurs there. In fact, this is exactly how James Baldwin reacted the first time he looked down on Georgia while looking out the window of an airplane: "I could not suppress the thought . . . that this earth had acquired its color from the blood that had dripped down from those trees" (Dray xi).

Recognizing the relationship between this poem and the play is crucial. Without establishing the fact that this poem interlocks with *The Barrier*, Hughes's intentions for it are unclear.[6] However, in reconnecting this text with this opera, we see that the themes of sexual desire and lynching can be read as key frames for the poem. Hughes's poem is careful to suggest that the symbol of "blood" (used three times in just twelve lines) is connected to "Everyone" (8). "Georgia Dusk" implies what no news article would dare to suggest: everyone is affected by lynching, not just the victim.

"Mississippi"

The practice of using various artistic mediums as a counternarrative is an important prelude to reading the poem "Mississippi." Hughes avoids naming the victim of a lynching in the final 1967 version of "Mississippi." This choice is particularly complex and very illuminating. Why would Hughes respond to the highly publicized lynching of Emmett Till by referencing the state in which it occurred rather than by directly mentioning Till by name? To answer this question, we must turn our attention back to the original version of this poem, which Hughes had written twelve years earlier in his own response to the murder of Emmett Till.

I will follow the consistently insightful research of Christopher Metress into the topic of how Hughes responded to the lynching of Till. Metress's research unknowingly begins the arduous process of reconstructing the fact that Hughes's poem serves as an important counternarrative. As many now know, fourteen-year-old Emmett Till was a black youth from Chicago who was vacationing in the summer of 1955 with his extended family who lived near Money, Mississippi. After allegedly whistling at the white clerk working in the local store, Till was kidnapped and beaten. His body was found six days later. His face was bloated and horrifically disfigured when it was recovered from the Tallahatchie River. He had been shot in the head, and a large cotton-gin wheel had been secured around his neck with barbed wire. Recent testimony has documented that Till was also castrated (Apel and Smith 62). Although two white men were acquitted of the murder, each later admitted in full detail that they had indeed committed the deed. The 2005 documentary *The Untold Story of Emmett Louis Till* asserts that as many as fourteen people may have been involved in the crime.

Equally important to the African American community, the body was placed on display in full open casket during the funeral back in Chicago, and extensive images of Till's face were published in *Jet* magazine. As many as 250,000 people may have viewed the body as it lay in the casket. The impact of Till's death was enormous. When Rosa Parks refused to give up her seat on a bus only three months later, "she related her decision to the shock of seeing the photographs of Emmett Till" (Apel and Smith 64). In fact, "many historians now argue that the modern civil rights movement was inspired by the protests that erupted across the country in the wake of Till's murder" (Goldsby 294). Till was not literally lynched from a tree by a rope, yet the fact that his death was consistently called a lynching suggests how this term continued to be expanded as it was used to refer to an ever-widening category of injustice.

As Metress has brilliantly and exhaustively traced, Hughes was the first African American to respond in writing to the lynching of Emmett Till. Metress notes that the first recorded appearance of the poem Hughes wrote in response to the lynching of Emmett Till was dated September 16, 1955. It appeared as a sort of headnote to a newspaper article written by Hughes and directed to the primarily black readers of the *Chicago Defender*. This article blurs together genres of editorial journalism, news coverage, and poetry. Hughes also addresses Congress's inability to investigate lynchings. The poem's text is also very unstable, as it varied in form depending upon its revision in multiple publications. Its intimate connection with the *Chicago Defender* warrants contextualizing it as a counternarrative to typical mainstream print coverage.

At one point, the poem became titled "Mississippi—1955" with the added dedication (To the Memory of Emmett Till). Given our understating of the censorship and cultural pressures surrounding Hughes in 1959, the reason why the poem did not appear in *Selected Poems* becomes more clear. There are measurable consequences to not being able to collect and republish such valuable material. The contents and longevity of Hughes's *Selected Poems* and *The Langston Hughes Reader* are very much part of the reason that there has been insufficient discussion of this poem. Indeed, Hughes's poems demand to be read within a cultural context as Hughes has so rightly been called "the prosecutor's star witness against American formalism and New Criticism" (Scott 107).

There are other reasons why this poem has not received more discussion. As Metress carefully uncovers, Hughes himself greatly revised this poem so that Till's name is completely absent from its final version, which appeared in *The Panther and the Lash* (1967). The failure of readers to acknowledge the presence of Till in the poem is "tied in great part to the decisions Hughes made to write Till out of the poem" (Metress 147). However, with much gratitude for his insight and research, I would like to respectfully but emphatically suggest that Till is not absent from the final version of the poem. Rather, two of Hughes's carefully placed time referents in the poem suggest his careful judgments in regard to how to best contextualize the lynching of Emmett Till. Further layers overlap with this poem, and these layers are in need of amplification.

The recurring use of autocitation in the poem is helpful for reconstructing this poem. Hughes consistently repeats the word "again" in the beginning of the poem. This repetition survives even in the final 1967 version: "terror comes again / To Mississippi. / *Again?*" (6–8). Hughes is engaging in the practice of autocitation by alluding to ideas first expressed in his own published poetry. His repeated idea of this happening "again" turns into his own italicized question: "*Again?*" A reader who wonders when such an event happened before in Mississippi need look no further than Hughes's own poetry. In "The Bitter River," Hughes laments the lynching of Charlie Lang and Ernest Green, who were hung from a bridge in Mississippi in 1942. "Again" is an example of autocitation in "Mississippi," which turns our attention to this earlier poem. This directive asserts that only the names and the ages have changed since the date almost thirteen years earlier when Charlie and Ernest were lynched. They were lynched, and nothing was done about it. As all three of these victims were teenage boys, it is also imperative that we consider Hughes's own fearsome journey through Texas at the age of eighteen as an experience that led him to express the fullest measure of empathy for these young male victims.

"Again" reminds us that Hughes finds himself again writing in response to a lynching. He points to these ideas as much as he does in the original newspaper column in which the poem first appeared. Hughes began the column by "connecting Till's death to the lynching of Charlie Lang and Ernest Green . . . [then] spent the remainder of the column skewering Congress for failing to investigate southern lynching" (Metress 141). Here multiple images are collapsed together. Hughes's longtime desire to counter the repeated failures to pass antilynching legislation turns toward an ironic counter to HUAC as he implies the compelling need for congressional investigation into the very un-American activity of lynching U.S. citizens. Moreover, his own poem "The Bitter River" as well as his own public appearance before HUAC only two years earlier are compressed.

The second example of autocitation in the 1967 version of the poem comes in the second-to-last line. Hughes states that "tears and blood / Still mix like rain / In Mississippi" (18–20). Metress's research leaves both its writer and readers wondering why Hughes would respond to the highly publicized lynching of Emmett Till by referencing the state in which it occurred rather than by directly mentioning Till by name. The answer becomes quite clear when we consider the important time referent Hughes settles on in line 19 of the poem when he says "Still." Hughes's poem is collapsing time rather than portraying specific events as "new" as a typical newspaper account might.

We must also remember that Hughes has already demonstrated the ability to respond to specific historical events with more generalized poetic ideas, as he is more poet than historian. For example, "Christ in Alabama" was written in response to the arrests of the Scottsboro Boys when no lynching occurred. Hughes's technique involved giving individual experiences collective meanings. Again, individual experiences get recontextualized in Hughes's poems to take on more expansive collective meanings. This collective meaning is the best means for discussing

Hughes's choice: Hughes's use of the word "Still" in "Mississippi" does not write Till out of the poem; instead, it writes all the other unknown lynch victims who have died in Mississippi back into the poem. This concept is fueled by Hughes's metaphor of "mixing" in the poem, which is an amplification of this same idea mentioned in "The Bitter River." The idea of mixing is forever captured in the word "Still." The last four letters are the last name of Emmett Till, and the opening s can be read as a quiet sibilant representing all the other nameless victims of lynching who hail from Mississippi. The letter s, so redundant in the state name Mississippi, is an appropriate figurative representation of those nameless victims who have died quietly throughout this state.

Such a reading explains a great deal. As Metress has documented, black writers such as Gwendolyn Brooks, James Baldwin, Toni Morrison, and others responded specifically to the lynching of Till. Unlike these other writers as well as many of the honorable men and women who have done such noble work preserving the important memory of Till, Hughes's response takes shape within the context of his own lifelong campaign against lynching and amid the reality that Till was only one of the many lynch victims who died in Mississippi. Hughes did not write about Till's lynching as an isolated incident; it took on a greater, collective meaning that certainly included Green, Lang, and other lynch victims.

Creating collective meaning has even more telling implications for current studies of Hughes and Till. Hughes's poetic response refuses to treat Till's murder as an isolated incident. Hughes decenters Till to use his death as a means to memorializing the others who were lynched without funerals, press coverage, and responses printed on the front pages of newspapers. Again, Hughes critiques the reception of such print coverage. It must be acknowledged that Hughes regarded the lynching of Till as more than an isolated incident. As such, Hughes used this incident as an opportunity to draw attention to the rest of Mississippi's nameless lynch victims.

Honest confusion about Hughes's apparent elimination of Till from the poem is a measurable representation of the effects of deinstitutionalizing images, discussions, and documents about American lynching culture. Moreover, it reminds us of how much there is to understand about Hughes's continual poetic responses to American lynching culture. Sadly, this deinstitutionalization continues. The collective ignorance in reducing Till's murder to an event that happened one time to one man in Mississippi during 1955 reveals a great deal about our still emerging understanding of both this important strain of Hughes's poetry and American lynching culture itself.

Hughes's word choice of "still" in this poem brings our discussion of Hughes's "The Negro" and "Mississippi" full circle. The word "still" in "Mississippi" interanimates his contemporaneous line revision in "The Negro." Given the powerful weight ascribed to the word "still," the poem collapses the distance between the 1942 lynchings of Charlie Lang and Ernest Green, the 1955 lynching of Emmett Till, and all the other unknown lynch victims who died in Mississippi. "Still" is the verbal cue that connects "The Bitter River," "The Negro," and "Mississippi." All three references to lynching overlap when Hughes chooses to revise line 16 of "The Negro" for his 1959 *Selected Poems* to read: "They lynch me still in Mississippi." In this revision, Hughes chooses to broaden our perspective of American lynching culture rather than to isolate specific victims. This word also adds another layer of depth to Hughes's choice to begin his 1962 public reading at the national poetry festival in Washington, D.C., with the poem "Still Here." Despite his own figurative lynching before HUAC years before where the committee had tried to make him "Stop laughin,' stop lovin,' stop livin,'" (6), Hughes was leaving a record for his perceptive listeners that he and his antilynching poems were "still here!" (8).

Hughes undermines print culture and negotiates censorship by appearing only to be retelling history in his poetic texts. Today, such a counternarrative allows us the opportunity to critique the reliability of the articles received by readers. Hughes not only passed lynching poems by retelling history, his counternarratives now offer us a chance to hear untold history. Perhaps in our search for history we find only stories. If so, the story of lynching is best told by literature, not newsprint sources. Hughes enacted this critique by negotiating and thus subverting the burdens placed on him through the mass production of ideas associated with publication. As a result, the use of the word "still" in "The Negro" passed. Our recognition of its importance reaffirms Hughes's persistence in his campaign against American lynching culture during a period when power sought to extinguish his defiance. Although many readers and listeners were unaware, Hughes was "still" writing about lynching.

Conclusion

In a historic speech delivered on March 15, 1965, President Lyndon Johnson announced to the world, "We shall overcome." By quoting the refrain from a well-known anthem, Johnson had unequivocally linked the goals of the dominant culture with those of the civil rights movement. In the wake of this triumphant speech, many things changed. One of these changes came over a year later, in November 1966, when Hughes's publishers at Knopf decided that "the times demanded" a "book of poems about racial wrongs and civil rights" (Rampersad 2: 409). Shortly after Hughes's death in 1967, Knopf published *The Panther and the Lash*. Only two years earlier, Knopf had refused to publish such a collection.

The times had finally begun to change, and many of Hughes's most important antilynching poems were presented in this mainstream collection. Against the backdrop of the Black Panther Party formed that same year, Hughes invoked the image of the "lash" in his title. The term "lash" suggests at least two things: it reminds us of the backlash Hughes had encountered from the dominant culture as it attempted to silence him, and, given the cultural framework established here, it activates one of the oldest definitions of lynching, which included, for a man found to be a horse thief, receiving thirty-nine lashes with a whip. Both meanings are significant. As relates to the first definition, Hughes finally was able to publish many of his statements about racial violence in a major literary collection. Sadly, Hughes did not quite outlive the forces of conservative censorship aimed against him. In regard to the physical violence implied by the word "lash," many of the powerful statements included in this collection were responses to lynchings. After Hughes spent a long period negotiating censorship, his collection strikes back against these forces.

However, these lynching poems appear with a clear sense of belatedness, which was highlighted by Hughes's dedication of the collection to Rosa Parks. The dedication turns our attention back to 1955, the year of Emmitt Till's death, an event that Parks cited as giving her the strength to protest being asked to move from her bus seat. In less visible ways, Hughes's poems against lynching had also been an important part of this struggle. Hughes's works, like Parks's protest, serve as similar touchstones for the long-standing fight that was sustained before the culminating work of the civil rights movement of the 1960s. Rather than serving as calls to further action, the poems lack much of their original force. They read like reminders of past battles.

Although *The Panther and the Lash* was published shortly after his death, Hughes himself selected the poems that were included. Hughes's choices in regard to revision, placement, and selection of poems highlight many of the means by which he conducted his campaign against American lynching culture. With their appearance in *The Panther and the Lash*, the poems we have been discussing take on an additional resonance of meaning.

►•◄

Hughes must have felt relieved to find himself facing a newfound freedom afforded him by a cultural climate now open to discussion of racial injustice. As a result, Hughes's final collection had no need to include poems about lynching that Hughes had previously been forced to pass. Because "The Negro Speaks of Rivers" and "The Negro" muted Hughes's varying commentary on racial violence, these poems were less important statements in the context of the late 1960s. Each of these poems had essentially already passed into print during a time where self-reassurance was necessary and censorship had to be avoided. Because Hughes could be more assertive in this collection, the project reflects more overt statements about lynching. Emotional modes of assurance and negotiation were no longer necessary for addressing lynching. Hence, the absence of these poems in this collection actually highlights the earlier constraints Hughes faced in having to pass his poetry.

While the aforementioned "The Negro" was no longer needed in *The Panther and the Lash*, the poem nonetheless contains ideas that serve as an important inflection in another poem included in the collection, "Mississippi." As we have seen, the word "still" in Hughes's "Mississippi" carries with it connotations from "The Negro." It offers a visual reminder of how lynching shifted topographically in Hughes's consciousness from Texas to Mississippi. Even in their absence, Ernest Green, Charlie Lang, and the countless unnamed and unacknowledged lynch victims remain memorialized in Hughes's most important poetic counternarrative to the lynching of Emmett Till. As Hughes himself wrote about this collection, the poems are about "the lives of people he has known, loved, and cried for, and the continual pall of racial smog that envelopes America" (Rampersad 2: 410).

Another poem in this collection is titled "Harlem." "Harlem" was also the original title of "Dream Deferred" when it first appeared in *Montage of Dream Deferred* (1951). The new "Harlem" in *The Panther and the Lash* is filled with autocitation as Hughes makes specific references to ideas first enunciated in "The Bitter River." In the new poem "Harlem," he writes of remembering "the old 'Be patient' / They told us before" (5–6). In this very short poem of only twenty-three lines, Hughes uses the word "remember" four times. The idea of "remembering" and being told to "be patient" are central ideas expressed in Hughes's antilynching poem of 1942 titled "The Bitter River." Conscious of this link, "The Bitter River" itself offers a striking parallel to "Dream Deferred" as Hughes writes here that America has "strangled my dream" (16). The echoes of "The Bitter River" can be found in another poem in this collection as well. Rather than speaking as a member of the military asked to fight in Vietnam, Hughes's speaker in "Militant" is prepared to fight for racial justice in America. He tells us that his anger is fueled in part by a terrible "bitterness in my throat" (5). Rather than remembering the pain of lynching as in "The Bitter River," this bitterness fuels anger to the pitch of violent retaliation.

"Dream Deferred"

The placement of "Dream Deferred" in *The Panther and the Lash* again animates the subject of lynching. Just as the image of crucifixion immediately preceded "Dream Deferred" when it appeared directly after "Not for Publication" a year earlier in *La Poésie Negro-Americaine*, here lynching is mentioned twice in "Death in Yorkville," the poem that immediately follows "Dream Deferred." "Death in Yorkville" chronicles the shooting of James Powell. The fifteen-year-old Powell was shot by a police officer. This officer mistakenly believed Powell was armed, and Powell drew his attention merely by walking through an upper-class area of Yorkville in Manhattan. The rioting that ensued was also noted by Hughes as he published "Harlem Call: After the 1964 Riots" (1964). The murder was highly significant to Hughes as he personally "joined thousands of other mourners at the viewing for Powell, which was held in Harlem in a funeral parlor only a few blocks from Hughes's home" (Rampersad 2: 690).

"Death in Yorkville" uses the death of Powell to suggest in its third stanza that black oppression has simply progressed through the shackles of slavery and lynching nooses to the current trend of shooting blacks. Although it is a shooting, Hughes asks how many years it takes to "Rope my neck—lynch me" (7). For Hughes's speaker, the bullets that killed Powell offer only another form of the oppression that began with the chains of slavery and continued through the act of lynching. While not excused by Hughes, perhaps rioting is an understandable reaction, given that the community's patience is overworn. Speaking in 1964, Hughes himself stated as much when he linked the current rioting with the past and present atrocities of lynching: "the blood extends from an average of two lynchings a week in the South a half century ago to an average of one violent and unsolved black death a week in Dixie today" (Clarke 215). According to the logic in "Death in Yorkville," the shooting of James Powell marked yet another of the newest forms of lynching. Among other things, trying to escape being murdered was an unspoken desire buried deep in the hearts of each member of Harlem. It was one of the promises implied in the dream of reaching the North. Not only have the memories of lynching culture followed them, they have remerged in new forms.

The shooting of James Powell is one example of a dream deferred. It is significant that this shooting, like so many others, is framed against the history of lynching in America. Given substantial artistic liberty in 1966 and 1967, Hughes placed "Dream Deferred" immediately adjacent to poems that addressed lynching, activating our awareness of the possible relationship between his subject and the poem.

"Death in Yorkville" concludes a long line of poems written in remembrance of black youths who were killed. While it is apparent that teenagers were often lynch victims, Hughes still has an unusually high number of poems dedicated to them. He mourned the Scottsboro Boys in "Christ in Alabama" and other poems; he memorialized teenagers Charlie Lang and Ernest Green in "The Bitter River"; he responded to the lynching of Emmett Till immediately with "Mississippi." Perhaps these compositions are a reflection of his ability to empathize with teenagers who died nearest the age Hughes himself was when he first encountered American lynching culture and reassured himself by writing "The Negro Speaks of Rivers" as he traveled through Texas at the age of eighteen.

This concern for the death of young people is coupled with the extended definition of lynching developed in the early 1950s in this collection as well. Hughes linked lynching with bombing in two poems in this collection. "Birmingham Sunday" recounts the September 15, 1963, church bombing in Birmingham, Alabama, that resulted in the deaths of four girls. "Bombings in Dixie" places such racial aggression in more general terms, reminding us, just as in "Mississippi," that there are many more bombings than the ones that get covered by newsprint.

Perhaps the most significant sequence in *The Panther and the Lash* comes in the first two poems of section three. This section, entitled "The Bible Belt," begins with "Christ in Alabama" and then is immediately followed by the poem formally known as "Not for Publication." Now titled "Bible Belt," Hughes's poem interanimates both the title of the section of the book as well as the word "lash" featured in the collection's title. "Bible Belt" certainly designates an area of the South, but it is reactivated here as the abuse inflicted on blacks by dominant culture. The title suggests that African Americans in this region are figuratively "lashed" by the area's religious conservatives.

Unlike the context surrounding the appearance of "Not for Publication" in both 1953 or 1959, a less ambiguous reading of the final three lines of Hughes's newly titled poem "Bible Belt" emerges in *The Panther and the Lash*. Published outside the cultural constraints of censorship, the dropping of the title "Not for Publication" places less emphasis on talking about racism and more on human beings being actual victims of lynching. Addressing censorship seemed anachronistic at a time when Hughes was enjoying the chance to publish poems about such racial issues. In this sequence, "Christ in Alabama" first establishes the imagery of crucifixion. "Bible Belt" immediately activates the same imagery by referencing "Jesus" in its first line. Hence, Hughes's final three lines in the poem assert that an imaginary black Christ would return only to be denied the right to pray in southern churches. However, as bad as that seems, current citizens of this part of the country can be crucified or lynched. This emphasis is noted visually as Hughes italicizes the word "*You.*" In other words, a black Christ would not be allowed to pray, but *You*, being even less important than He, can be lynched.

Rather than being figuratively lynched for speaking about racism, the muscular flexibility of the former "Not for Publication" now emphasizes what happens to those who live in the South. The change of title, shift in cultural context, and sequencing here move the emphasis away from the dangers of publishing about racism and toward racism itself. To Hughes's speaker, worshiping race rather than faith allows churches to bask in the multiple criteria that make their South topophilic as integration has been resisted, and lynching culture has sustained their status of superiority. For the Black Christ and literal black citizens, this place's topophobia is intensified by violence and frustrated by religious hypocrisy. For them, the Bible Belt is known more for enacting crucifixion than for following the lessons of its most celebrated victim.

While the publication of *The Panther and the Lash* marked a rare moment in time when many of Langston Hughes's lynching poems made their way into a mainstream collection, these same poems have not fared so well in being incorporated into many of our educational institutions. One important element of this study that remains to be addressed is trying to locate exactly where a discussion of Langston Hughes's lynching poetry belongs. Can it be successfully incorporated into high school English classes? Some may suggest that this subject matter, accompanying photography and descriptions of sadistic torture, may be better suited for college classrooms. If so, in which departments will it be taught—American history, American studies, or English departments? Given the emerging lenses of literary criticism in the relationship between geography, culture, and poetry, opportunities for continuing to explore tensions between art, politics, and race are still necessary in African American studies, critical race studies, and American literature. Wherever lynching continues to emerge as a topic for critical discourse, Langston Hughes's poetry stands ready for consideration.

Another generation of citizens should not be able to ignore American lynching culture. There are no more sufficient alibis. The harsh realities of lynching must continue to become engrafted to our educational institutions. As the speaker in "The Bitter River" reminds us, there is always the burden to remember. Remembering should happen formally through educational training, not just orally via cultural memory. Our institutions owe their students a deep and well-informed cultural understanding of the reality that thousands of African Americans were dismembered, tortured, murdered, and literally divided into separate parts to be sold as souvenirs. This is why the public display of a noose is so offensive. This is why the relationship between legal verdicts, capital punishment, and lynching is so important to continue to revisit. The possible connections between lynching and some of the intimidation strategies implemented in our international prisons requires that we recognize and, if necessary, refuse to initiate the strategies refined by American lynching culture as they emerge in new forms. Lynching is still relevant. It informs the privileges some enjoy by being coded "white" as this racial category was at least partially invented through the unity created among different ethnic groups as they cast aside differences to focus on skin color during the corporate act of lynching blacks.

What we learn from lynching is that it has a significant cultural impact on instigators and victims, not all of whom physically participate at the lynching site. Consensus, observation, awareness, and acceptance penetrate to the deepest levels of American society. This happens in differing degrees to victims, participants, or people who imagine they are sheltered by apathy or indifference. The history of lynching in America tells us something about where we are and where we have been. There seems little doubt that its energies are continually transforming and reemerging.

There is great dignity and power to be found in Langston Hughes's varying modes of personal and poetic resistance. Hughes's lynching poetry offers a counternarrative to press clippings, a demonstration of personal and literary passing, the strength found in reassurance, the indignation toward the injustice that fueled his anger, and complex strategies for negotiating censorship. At a time when he could not say, he showed that expanded definitions of lynching were necessary. Hughes's poetic works leave us sifting the cultural remainders of one modern writer's topophilic and topophobic relationship with America.

Notes

Introduction

1. Although I focus on the impact lynching had on these African American men, the historian Nell Irvin Painter reminds us that lynch victims also included "some women and children, that other Americans also were victims, notably Mexicans, but also white people, including white women." For more information, see Democracy Now, "Senate Apologizes for Not Enacting Anti-Lynching Legislation: A Look at Journalist and Anti-Lynching Crusader Ida B. Wells," www.democracy now.org/ 2005/6/14/senate_apologizes_for_not_enacting_anti.

Chapter 1. The Red Summer of 1919: Finding Reassurance

1. For more information on lynching statistics for Texas, see James M. SoRelle, "Jesse Washington Lynching," The Handbook of Texas Online, University of Texas at Austin, www.tsha.utexas.edu/handbook/online/articles/view/JJ/jcjl.html.

2. Further information on NAACP membership can be found in Michael L. Gillette, "National Association for the Advancement of Colored People," The Handbook of Texas Online, University of Texas at Austin, www.tsha.utexas.edu/handbook/online/articles/view/NN/ven1.html.

3. More information about the "Waco horror" can be located in James M.

SoRelle, "Jesse Washington Lynching," The Handbook of Texas Online, University of Texas at Austin, www.tsha.utexas.edu/handbook/online/articles/view/JJ/jcjl. html.

4. The events surrounding Samuel L. Jones and Calvin P. Davis are described in Ken Durham, "Longview Race Riot of 1919," The Handbook of Texas Online, University of Texas at Austin, www.tsha.utexas.edu/handbook/online/articles/view/LL/jcl2/html.

5. The illustration of the man being burned can be found in the December 1910 issue of *Crisis* (15); "The National Pastime" appeared in the January 1911 *Crisis* (18–19); and the reference to Great Britain's lack of lynchings is from the February 1911 *Crisis* (14).

6. See the inside covers of the December 1918 and February 1919 *Crisis* for these full-page advertisements promoting the work of the NAACP.

7. The story reported by the Houston branch can be found in *Crisis*, February 1919, 182. For the report on the revival of the Klan in Texas, see *Crisis*, March 1919, 229. The two-page lynching summary can be found in *Crisis*, February 1919, 180–81.

8. More information on the events in Arkansas can be found in Richard Wormser, "Red Summer," Jim Crow Stories, Public Broadcasting Service, www.pbs.org/wnet/jimcrow/stories_events_red.html. For more about the incident at Wilmington, see Richard Wormser, "Wilmington Riots," Jim Crow Stories, Public Broadcasting Service, www.pbs.org/wnet/jimcrow?stories_events_riot.html.

9. For further philosophical analysis of the relationship between memory and active participation with nature, see Barfield, *Saving the Appearances*.

10. See Green, *Black Women Composers* 52–53, for more about Margaret Bonds's composition of Hughes's "The Negro Speaks of Rivers." See also Berry, *Langston Hughes* 248, for information about Marian Anderson's performance of Hughes's poem; Berry's text also notes the postcards Hughes sent out to friends (300) and makes mention of his film proposal (305).

Chapter 2. The Scottsboro Case and World War II America: Poetic Anger

1. To view each of Taylor's three different lithographs for the cover as well as the others I discuss in this chapter that were included in *Scottsboro Limited*, see Rose and Quiroz's *The Lithographs of Prentiss Taylor*, 68, 69, 77, 78.

2. See Rice, *Witnessing Lynching* 271, for a photograph of Ruby Bates appearing with the mothers of the Scottsboro Boys on Mother's Day, May 14, 1934, in Washington, D.C.

3. One example is Hughes's letter addressed to Guy B. Johnson, 31 October 1933, series 2.1, box 8, folders 110–131, Guy B. Johnson Papers #3826, Wilson Library, University of North Carolina at Chapel Hill.

4. See Wells-Barnett, *On Lynchings*, for a statistical analysis of the surprisingly low number of lynchings committed in response to accusations of rape.

5. Hughes read his poems in Gerrard Hall. In *The Life of Langston Hughes*, this building is mistakenly identified by its architectural features as the "Greek Revival Little Theater" (1: 225). Moreover, *The Life of Langston Hughes* suggests that Hughes made another appearance at the University of North Carolina at Chapel Hill in the winter of 1960 (2: 309); however, no record of such an appearance exists in the university's archives, although appearances by Robert Frost, Kenneth Rexroth, Roy Wilkins, Andres Segovia, Ray Charles, and Martin Luther King Jr. are noted.

6. In a letter dated November 25, 1931, Johnson wrote about sending Hughes these funds and about Hughes leaving Chapel Hill. Hughes confirmed receiving the funds in a letter dated December 3, 1931. These two letters, along with a list of contributors to Hughes's fund and the reasons Johnson listed for having difficulty in securing funds mentioned in an unsent letter addressed to Hughes can be located in a letter dated 25 November 1931, series 2.1, box 8, folders 110–131, Guy B. Johnson Papers #3826, Wilson Library, University of North Carolina at Chapel Hill.

7. I thank Biff Hollingsworth, who brought these materials to my attention, as well as Laura White for locating, securing, and documenting this information from series 2.1, box 8, folders 110–131, Guy B. Johnson Papers #3826, Wilson Library, University of North Carolina at Chapel Hill.

8. This statement by David Clark appeared in the October 2 1932, *Charlotte Observer*. The article is located in series 2.1, box 8, folders 110–131, Guy B. Johnson Papers #3826, Wilson Library, University of North Carolina at Chapel Hill

9. This poem appeared in print in several forms under the titles "Youth" and "Poem." This is the only time Hughes used the title "Tomorrow" for this poem. Hughes's inclusion of this final line takes on a tone of socialist protest here against the injustices perpetrated on the Scottsboro Boys. Later, in yet another slightly different form, Hughes's final lines reprinted in the 1958 *Langston Hughes Reader* lose their tone of communist aggression as they are contextualized much differently within the protests of the civil rights era.

10. Information on the university's statement regarding free speech, Johnson's request to distribute poems, Hughes's written reply, and copies of the four autographed poems are located in series 2.1, box 8, folders 110–131, Guy B. Johnson Papers #3826, Wilson Library, University of North Carolina at Chapel Hill.

11. Locating a copy of Cullen's "Christ Recrucified" can be arduous; see Rice, *Witnessing Lynching*, 221–22 for a complete version of the poem.

12. The Shubuta Bridge was added to the National Register of Historic Sites on November 16, 1988; it is listed as site #88002490.

Chapter 3. Negotiating Censorship in the 1950s: Lynching as Analogy

1. The PBS broadcast *Freedom Never Dies* (2001) led Florida attorney general Charlie Crist to reopen Harry Moore's case. Crist concluded that KKK leaders Earl

Brooklyn, Tillman Belvin, Joseph Cox, and Edward Spivey killed the Moores. By this time, all four men were deceased.

2. See *The Life of Langston Hughes*, vol. 2, for Hughes's attempts to cast Robeson in Hughes's 1941 movie script *The Songs of Solomon Jones* (29). On June 27, 1943, Robeson starred in Hughes's short radio play *John Henry Hammers It Out*, broadcast in New York (71). Hughes also drafted a play for the BBC in 1944 entitled *The Ballad of the Man Who Went to War*, in which Robeson was set to star.

3. For more on Hughes's relationship with Henri Cartier-Bresson, see his descriptions in *I Wonder as I Wander* of their time in Mexico (*CW* 14: 287), celebration of Bastille Day in Paris (*CW* 14: 310–11), and Christmas celebration in Paris (*CW* 14: 383).

4. Hughes's collaborative articles with Griffith J. Davis, all appearing in *Ebony*, include one on Harlem entertainers (March 1949, 36–38), another on Harlem's churches (May 1949, 47, 49–50), and another on Atlanta (January 1948, 19–24).

5. This quote can be found in Palfi's *Invisible in America*. Because Palfi's text is not paginated, I cite either the section of the book in which the information can be found or the nearest numbered plate.

6. For more on Hughes's statements about photography, see his unpublished "Pictures More Than Pictures: The Work of Manuel Bravo and Cartier-Bresson," March 6, 1935, in box 329, folder 5369, Langston Hughes Papers, Beinecke Library, Yale University.

Chapter 4. Poetry as Counternarrative: Retelling History

1. For more on the practice of removing the right hands of citizens who could not pay a labor tax under the reign of King Leopold, see Babb, *Historical Dictionary of Zaire* 55.

2. These seven new poems were "Tambourines," "As Befits a Man," "Maybe," "Blue Monday," "To Artina," "Uncle Tom," and "Jim Crow Car."

3. This comment is located on a draft of "Tambourines" held in the James Weldon Johnson Collection, Beinecke Library, Yale University.

4. For a complete account of this lynching, see Ginzburg, *100 Years of Lynching* 236–38.

5. Mobs often lynched relatives when the primary suspect could not be found. For example, Laura Nelson was lynched from a bridge above the Canadian River near Okemah, Oklahoma, on May 25, 1911. Laura and her son L. W. were arrested and jailed immediately after L. W. shot a deputy who was searching for the boy's father. The father was later secured in a federal penitentiary on charges of stealing cattle. Unable to lynch the father, the mob settled on Laura and L. W.

6. Although it does not appear in *The Barrier*, Hughes's poem "Flight" also bears unexpected similarities to this plotline. Published in *Opportunity* in 1930, "Flight" was written at the same time that Hughes was completing the script for

Mulatto. The poem depicts, in eight short lines, the attempted escape of someone who appears to be facing accusations of rape as he runs to avoid being lynched. Like many of the examples discussed here, Bert is told to find his way to the swamp to avoid being detected by bloodhounds. In fact, this same theme appears in Hughes's 1942 play *The Sun Do Move* as the main characters, named Frog and Rock, take a similar route of escape.

Bibliography

Allen, James. *Without Sanctuary: Lynching Photography in America*. Santa Fe: Twin Palms, 2000.

"Along the N.A.A.C.P. Battlefront." *Crisis* (March 1953): 168–69.

Apel, Dora. *Imagery of Lynching: Black Men, White Women, and the Mob*. New Brunswick, N.J.: Rutgers University Press, 2004.

Apel, Dora, and Shawn Michelle Smith. *Lynching Photographs*. Berkley and Los Angeles: University of California Press, 2007.

Axelrod, Steve, Camille Roman, and Thomas Travisano. "Langston Hughes." In *The New Anthology of American Poetry*, vol. 2. New Brunswick, N.J.: Rutgers University Press, 2005.

Babb, F. Scott. *Historical Dictionary of Zaire*. London: Scarecrow Press, 1988.

Banks, Kimberley. "'Like a violin for the wind to play': Lyrical Approaches to Lynching by Hughes, Du Bois, and Toomer." *African American Review* 38.3 (2004): 451–65.

Barfield, Owen. *Saving the Appearances: A Study of Idolatry*. New York: Harcourt, Brace and World, 1965.

Barker, Kenneth, ed. *NIV Study Bible*. Grand Rapids, Mich.: Zondervan, 1985.

Bennett, Michael. "Anti-Pastoralism, Frederick Douglass, and the Nature of Slavery." In *Beyond Nature Writing: Expanding the Bounds of Ecocriticism*, edited by Karla Armbruster and Kathleen R. Wallace, 195–210. Charlottesville: University Press of Virginia, 2001.

Berkowitz, George, to Marion Palfi. Typed memo. April 20, 1949. Center for Creative Photography, University of Arizona.

Bernstein, Patricia. *The First Waco Horror: The Lynching of Jesse Washington and the Rise of the NAACP*. College Station: Texas A&M University Press, 2005.

Berry, Faith. *Langston Hughes: Before and Beyond the Harlem Renaissance*. New York: Random House, 1996.

Blair, Sara. *Harlem Crossroads: Black Writers and the Photograph in the Twentieth Century*. Princeton: Princeton University Press, 2007.

Bontemps, Arna, and Langston Hughes. *Arna Bontemps–Langston Hughes Letters (1925–1967)*. Edited by Charles H. Nichols. New York: Dodd, Mead, 1980.

Buttitta, Tony. *The Lost Summer: A Personal Memoir of F. Scott Fitzgerald*. New York: St. Martin's Press, 1987.

Capeci, Dominic J. *The Lynching of Cleo Wright*. Lexington: University Press of Kentucky, 1998.

Carrigan, William D. *The Making of a Lynching Culture: Violence and Vigilantism in Central Texas, 1836–1916*. Urbana: University of Illinois Press, 2004.

Cartwright, Marguerite. "The Mob Still Rides—Tuskegee Notwithstanding." *Crisis* (April 1953): 222–23.

Civil Rights Congress. *We Charge Genocide: The Historic Petition to the United Nations for Relief from a Crime of the United States Government against the Negro People*. New York: International, 1951.

Clarke, John Henrik. *Harlem: A Community in Transition*. New York: Citadel Press, 1964.

Cullen, Countee. "Christ Recrucified." In *Witnessing Lynching: American Writers Respond*, edited by Anne P. Rice, 221–22. New Brunswick, N.J.: Rutgers University Press, 2003.

Cunard, Nancy Clara. "Scottsboro and Other Scottsboros." In *Witnessing Lynching: American Writers Respond*, edited by Anne P. Rice, 272–81. New Brunswick, N.J.: Rutgers University Press, 2003.

De Santis, Christopher. "The Essayistic Vision of Langston Hughes." In *Montage of a Dream Deferred: The Art and Life of Langston Hughes*, edited by John Edgar Tidwell and Cheryl R. Ragar, 284–304. Columbia: University of Missouri Press, 2007.

Dodd, Elizabeth. "The Great Rainbowed Swamp: History as Moral Ecology in the Poetry of Michael S. Harper." In *Beyond Nature Writing: Expanding the Boundaries of Ecocriticism*, edited by Karla Armbruster and Kathleen R. Wallace, 177–94. Charlottesville: University Press of Virginia, 2001.

Dos Passos, John. "Scottsboro's Testimony." *Contempo* 1.6 (1931): 1.

Douglas, Kelly Brown. *The Black Christ*. New York: Orbis Books, 1994.

Dray, Philip. *At the Hands of Persons Unknown: The Lynching of Black America*. New York: Random House, 2002.

Dreiser, Theodore. "Humanitarianism in the Scottsboro Case." *Contempo* 1.6 (1931): 1.

Duberman, Martin Bauml. *Paul Robeson*. New York: Knopf, 1988.

Enyeart, James L. "Director's Statement." In *Marion Palfi*, 3. Tucson: University of Arizona Press, 1983.

Geis, Gilbert, and Leigh B. Bienen. *Crimes of the Century: From Leopold and Loeb to O. J. Simpson*. Boston: Northeastern University Press, 1998.

Gilroy, Paul. *The Black Atlantic: Modernity and Double Consciousness*. Cambridge: Harvard University Press, 1993.

Ginzburg, Ralph. *100 Years of Lynching*. Baltimore: Black Classic Press, 1997.

Goldsby, Jacqueline. *A Spectacular Secret: Lynching in American Life and Literature*. Chicago: University of Chicago Press, 2006.

Green, Mildred Denby. *Black Women Composers: A Genesis*. Boston: Twayne, 1983.

Gussow, Adam. *Seems Like Murder Here: Southern Violence and the Blues Tradition*. Chicago: University of Chicago Press, 2002.

Hale, Grace Elizabeth. *Making Whiteness: The Culture of Segregation in the South, 1890–1940*. New York: Pantheon, 1998.

Harper, Donna Akiba Sullivan. *Not So Simple: The "Simple" Stories by Langston Hughes*. Columbia: University of Missouri Press, 1995.

Hughes, Langston. *The Collected Works of Langston Hughes*. Edited by Arnold Rampersad. 17 vols. Columbia: University of Missouri Press, 2001–4.

———. *Good Morning Revolution: Uncollected Writings of Social Protest*. Edited by Faith Berry. Secaucus: Carol Publishing Group, 1992.

———. *Remember Me to Harlem: The Letters of Langston Hughes and Carl Van Vechten 1925–1964*. Edited by Emily Bernard. New York: Knopf, 2001.

Jemie, Onwuchenkwa. "Or Does It Explode?" In *Langston Hughes: Critical Perspectives Past and Present*, edited by Henry Louis Gates Jr. and K. A. Appiah, 135–71. New York: Amistad, 1993.

Jongh, James de. "The Poet Speaks of Places: A Close Reading of Langston Hughes's Literary Use of Place." In *A Historical Guide to Langston Hughes*, edited by Steven C. Tracy, 65–84. Oxford: Oxford University Press, 2004.

Julien, Isaac. "'Black Is, Black Ain't': Notes on De-Essentializing Black Identity." In *Black Popular Culture*, edited by Gina Dent, 255–63. New York: New Press, 1983.

Kellner, Bruce. "Working Friendship: A Harlem Renaissance Footnote." In *The Lithographs of Prentiss Taylor*, edited by Ingrid Rose and Roderick S. Quiroz, 11–18. New York: Fordham University Press, 1996.

Keneally, Thomas. *Lincoln*. London: Weidenfeld and Nicolson, 2003.

Kim, Daniel Won-gu. "We, Too, Rise with You": Recovering Langston Hughes's African (Re)Turn 1954–1960 in *An African Treasury*, the *Chicago Defender*, and *Black Orpheus*. *African American Review* 41.3 (Fall 2007): 419–41.

King, Carol Weiss. "Facts about Scottsboro." *Contempo* 1.13 (1931): 1, 4.

Lewis, David Levering. *When Harlem Was in Vogue*. New York: Oxford University Press, 1989.

———. "Wounds Not Scars: Lynching, the National Conscience and the American Historian." *Journal of American History* 83 (March 1997): 1221–53.

Lindquist-Cock, Elizabeth. "Marion Palfi: An Appreciation." In *Marion Palfi*, 5–11. Tucson: University of Arizona Press, 1983.

Litwack, Leon F. Introduction to *Without Sanctuary: Lynching Photography in America*. Santa Fe: Twin Palms, 2000.

Loewen, James W. *Lies My Teacher Told Me: Everything Your American History Textbook Got Wrong*. New York: New Press, 1995.

Lutes, Jean M. "Lynching Coverage and the American Reporter-Novelist." *American Literary History* 19.2 (Summer 2007): 456–81.

"Lynching Report." *Crisis* (February 1953): 103.

Mason, Jerry D. *Shubuta Mississippi: Home of the Red Artesian Water*. Self-published, 2002.

Metress, Christopher. "Langston Hughes's 'Mississippi-1955': A Note on Revisions and an Appeal for Reconsideration." *African American Review* 37.1 (2003): 139–48.

Miller, R. Baxter. *The Art and Imagination of Langston Hughes*. Lexington: University Press of Kentucky, 1989.

Miller, W. Jason. "Justice, Lynching, and American Riverscapes: Finding Reassurance in Langston Hughes's 'The Negro Speaks of Rivers.'" *Langston Hughes Review* 18.1 (Spring 2004): 24–37.

Murray, Albert. *Stomping the Blues*. New York: De Capo Press, 1976.

"Negro Lecturer Gives Humorous History of Life." *Daily Tar Heel*, November 21, 1931, 1.

"Negro Poet Will Deliver Talk on Race Problems." *Daily Tar Heel*, November 19, 1931, 1.

Nevels, Cynthia Skove. *Lynching to Belong: Claiming Whiteness through Racial Violence*. College Station: Texas A&M University Press, 2007.

Osborn, Alice. "The Hanging Bridge of Shubuta, Mississippi—A Testimony to Trauma." Student paper, North Carolina State University, 2006.

Palfi, Marion. *Invisible in America: An Exhibition of Photographs by Marion Palfi*. Lawrence: University of Kansas Museum of Art, 1973.

Pinsker, Matthew. *Abraham Lincoln*. Washington, D.C.: CQ Press, 2002.

Ponce, Martin Joseph. "Langston Hughes's Queer Blues." *Modern Language Quarterly* 66.4 (December 2005): 505–37.

Rampersad, Arnold. *The Life of Langston Hughes*. 2 vols. New York: Oxford University Press, 2002.

Rice, Anne P. Introduction to *Witnessing Lynching: American Writers Respond*, edited by Rice. New Brunswick, N.J.: Rutgers University Press, 2003.

"The Riot at Longview, Texas." *Crisis* 18.6 (October 1919): 297–98.

Roman, Camille. *Elizabeth Bishop's World War II–Cold War View*. New York: Palgrave, 2001.

Roosevelt, Eleanor, to Steven Early. August 8, 1936. President's Personal File. Franklin D. Roosevelt Library, Hyde Park, N.Y.

———, to Walter White. March 19, 1936. NAACP Records. Library of Congress, Washington, D.C.

Rose, Ingrid, and Roderick S. Quiroz. *The Lithographs of Prentiss Taylor*. New York: Fordham University Press, 1996.

Rotnem, Victor W. "The Federal Civil Right 'Not to Be Lynched.'" In *Lynching in America: A History in Documents*, edited by Christopher Waldrep, 238–41. New York: New York University Press, 2006.

Sanders, Leslie Catherine. Introduction to *The Collected Works of Langston Hughes*, vol. 6, edited by Sanders with Nancy Johnston. Columbia: University of Missouri Press, 2001.

Scott, Jonathan. *Socialist Joy in the Writing of Langston Hughes*. Columbia: University of Missouri Press, 2006.

Shapiro, Herbert. *White Violence and Black Response: From Reconstruction to Montgomery*. Amherst: University of Massachusetts Press, 1988.

Smethurst, James. "The Adventures of a Social Poet: Langston Hughes from the Popular Front to Black Power." In *A Historical Guide to Langston Hughes*, edited by Steven C. Tracy, 141–68. Oxford: Oxford University Press, 2004.

Smith, Raymond. "Hughes: Evolution of the Poetic Persona." In *Modern Critical Views: Langston Hughes*, edited by Harold Bloom, 45–60. New York: Chelsea House, 1989.

Smith McKoy, Sheila. *When Whites Riot: Writing Race and Violence in American and South African Cultures*. Madison: University of Wisconsin Press, 2001.

Snyder, Robert E. "Without Sanctuary: An American Holocaust?" *Southern Quarterly* 39.3 (2001): 162–69.

Soto, Isabel. "The Empowerment of Displacement." In *Montage of a Dream Deferred: The Art and Life of Langston Hughes*, edited by John Edgar Tidwell and Cheryl R. Ragar, 169–80. Columbia: University of Missouri Press, 2007.

Spillers, Hortense J. "Mama's Baby, Papa's Maybe: An American Grammar Book." In *The Women and Language Debate: A Sourcebook*, edited by Camille Roman, Suzanne Juhasz, and Christine Miller, 56–77. New Brunswick, N.J.: Rutgers University Press, 1994.

Steffens, Lincoln. "Lynching by Law or by Lustful Mob, North and South: Red and Black." *Contempo* 1.13 (1931): 1.

Summers-Brenner, Eluned. "Unreal City and Dream Deferred." In *Geomodernisms*, edited by Laura Doyle and Laura Winkel, 262–80. Bloomington: Indiana University Press, 2005.

Thompson, Julius E. *Lynching in Mississippi: A History, 1865–1965*. London: McFarland, 2007.

Thurston, Michael. "Black Christ, Red Flag: Langston Hughes on Scottsboro." *College Literature* 22.3 (1995): 30–52.

———. "Montage of a Dream Destroyed." *Montage of a Dream Deferred: The Art and Life of Langston Hughes*, edited by John Edgar Tidwell and Cheryl R. Ragar, 195–208. Columbia: University of Missouri Press, 2007.

Tidwell, John Edgar, and Cheryl R. Ragar. Introduction to *Montage of a Dream Deferred: The Art and Life of Langston Hughes*, edited by Tidwell and Ragar. Columbia: University of Missouri Press, 2007.

Tracy, Steven C. *Langston Hughes and the Blues*. 1988. Urbana: University of Illinois Press, 2001.

Turner, Henry McNeal. *Respect Black: The Writings and Speeches of Henry McNeal Turner*. Edited by Edwin Redkey. New York: Arno Press, 1971.

"Tuskegee Report." *Hartford Courant*, December 31, 1953, 5.

United States. Executive Sessions of the Senate Permanent Subcommittee on Investigations of the Committee on Government Operations. *Hearings*. 83rd Cong., 1st sess. Washington, D.C.: GPO, 2003.

"The Waco Horror." *Crisis* 12.3 (July 1916): 1–8.

Wells-Barnett, Ida B. *On Lynchings*. Salem: Ayer, 1990.

White, George H. "Defense of the Negro Race—Charges Answered: Speech of Hon. George H. White, of North Carolina, in the House of Representatives, January 29, 1901." 31st Cong., 2nd sess. Washington: GPO, 1901. 1–14.

Whitman, Walt. "Crossing Brooklyn Ferry." In *American Literature: Tradition and Innovation*, vol. 2, edited by Harrison T. Meserole, Walter Sutton, and Brom Weber, 1917–22. Lexington: Raytheon Education Company, 1969.

Zall, Paul M., ed. *Lincoln on Lincoln*. Lexington: University Press of Kentucky, 1999.

Zangrando, Robert L. *The NAACP Crusade against Lynching, 1909–1950*. Philadelphia: Temple University Press, 1980.

Index

Page numbers in *italics* refer to illustrations.

W. Jason Miller is assistant professor in the Department
of English at North Carolina State University.